any other woman

[NEWEST PRESS]

any other woman
an uncommon biography

by Monica Kidd

[Copyright ©] Monica Kidd 2008

Library and Archives Canada Cataloguing in Publication
Kidd, Monica, 1972–
Any other woman / Monica Kidd.
Includes bibliographical references.
ISBN 978-1-897126-30-1
I. Title.
PS8571.I354A79 2008   C813'.6   C2008-902612-8

Editor for the Board: Michael Penny
Text Editor: Carol Berger
Cover and interior design: Natalie Olsen
Cover photo: Natalie Olsen
Author photo: Steve Hunt

NeWest Press acknowledges the support of the Canada Council for the
Arts, the Alberta Foundation for the Arts, and the Edmonton Arts Council
for our publishing program. We also acknowledge the financial support of the
Government of Canada through the Book Publishing Industry Development
Program (BPIDP).

NeWest Press
201 8540 109 Street
Edmonton, Alberta T6G 1E6
(780) 432-9427
newestpress.com

No bison were harmed in the making of this book.
We are committed to protecting the environment and to the responsible use
of natural resources. This book is printed on 100% recycled, ancient forest-
friendly paper.

1 2 3 4 5 11 10 09 08

printed and bound in Canada

For all the women,
with their bags and betrothals.

Coal does not make us think of the rich,
but of the poor.
— Barbara Freese,
from *Coal: A Human History*

You don't need to know everything …
there are lit-up moments, and the rest is dark.
— Jeanette Winterson,
from *Lighthousekeeping*

[prologue]

One night, a man fell in love with a photograph.
The day's work draining from his crooked bones,
Andrew Zak held Rosalia up to a kerosene lamp,
saw surprise in her dark eyes,
and held her there a moment.
Then he passed her back to her uncle
and fell asleep,
dreaming of a bucket
that would not empty.

part one

[ch. one]

There is a family story which goes like this.

One night in the early hours of the twentieth century, a group of men, immigrants all, sat around a bunkhouse in a coalmine camp in the southern reaches of the Rocky Mountains. None was long off the boat, and everything was new. The mines had barely begun to open their black mouths. Alberta was an idea, the reality of which had not yet arrived.

The men in the bunkhouse passed the time telling stories of life at home. Andrew Zak was born a Slovak in the late nineteenth century. At the age of fourteen he quit school and went to work selling glass from a sack on his back. Early in his adult years, having already sweated through half a lifetime's worth of work, he heard about jobs in a place called the Crowsnest Pass, where a man could make five dollars a day and have food on the table and a place to sleep at night. He decided, like thousands of others, to go and try his luck.

Andrew had travelled much and taught himself many languages, making him a welcome companion on dark nights around a wooden table with a long day's work behind and nothing but the wind for company. The men passed around photos of their families. A picture of Rosalia Patala came to rest in Andrew's hands. The girl, her uncle explained, was working in New York City, cooking and cleaning for a wealthy family. She was alone and single. She too was from Slovakia. She would make someone a good wife. "You, Andrew. Maybe you."

Andrew wrote to the girl and proposed. Rosalia accepted. She left New York and began the train journey west to the Crowsnest Pass. But that's just a story. If it's true, where is my great-grandmother's train ticket? Where is the letter from her husband-to-be, which she must have read and folded until the paper was thin as a moth's wing? Where is the photo he held between his coal-blackened thumb and index finger (already shortened in one of a number of accidents), the photo he might have swapped for a flask of whiskey to keep him warm on the last long nights of bachelorhood?

Perhaps it is the prairie tendency to want to wiggle free of history that makes my family disinclined to keep such things as photos or letters. For all I know Andrew and Rosalia had no desires, took no wrong turns, had no second thoughts; they merely met, married, worked, came north in 1919 to the homestead, then stepped aside for successively noisy, busy generations with their pickup trucks and complicated families.

Nonsense.

On a shelf in what used to be my bedroom in my parents' house in Elnora, Alberta, I once found a thick blue photo album. Its plastic-covered sheets had begun to fuse with the diagonal strips of glue. There were snaps of my father playing baseball in the field beside the grain elevator, of him standing in his new grocery store wearing plaid polyester pants and a ball cap that matched the one worn by his friend beside him, of my placid grandmother with her cat-eye glasses, her hands folded before a visiting photographer's fake fireplace in a boardroom above the Credit Union. Lying between the pages I found a stiff paper photo, the size and texture of a large playing card. Its edges were torn where a Scotch tape border had been partly removed; the surface was folded and creased like the skin on someone's knuckle. I have a copy of it still.

Four people are gathered outside a finely boarded log cabin. There is snow on the ground. The cross-bars of a high iron bed are visible through the front window. A small girl with thin lips, suspicious eyes, and a fierce head of hair surrounding a plump face wears a high-necked black dress that falls below her knees; she hides her hands primly behind her back. Beside her, on her mother's lap, sits a smaller girl in a white dress, black boots, and striped woolen hat; her baby hands curl patiently at her belly, but her dark eyes look anxious. The mother, sitting heavily in a wooden chair, wears a coarse plaid skirt that rests on the ground, a high-necked white blouse, and a black jacket with puckered pleats at the shoulders. With the exception of one rogue curl at her right temple, her dark hair is swept high into a neat bun. Her hands are strong and knuckly — they could be my mother's. The father has large ears and a long, low nose. He stands to the left of his wife and is dressed in a grey striped shirt, a polka-dotted tie, and a five-button vest; one hand rests on the back of his wife's chair, the other on his older daughter's shoulder. The first joint of his index finger is missing.

The parents are Andrew and Rosalia. Emma Helen is their eldest, their first surviving child, my grandmother. The baby is Annie. Their first baby had died at the end of a few weeks of sickly life. Susie, Tom, and Mary will come later. A ninety-year-old photo, an old story, and the presence of their descendants is the only proof I have that they ever existed. The blank spaces in their narrative are like a long breath held.

[i]

*She floats on her back in the thick, green river,
eyes trained on the bottomless sky. Goose bumps
cover her arms and legs. Under her shift, her
worn nipples have puckered into tight, brown
rosebuds.*

*Nothing moves except her long hair and the
water, tugging eastward through brush fires and
mud and grasshoppers to Hudson's Bay. The air
cracks with August's heat.*

*From the shore, two tiny voices call to her.
She blinks and rolls onto her belly and dives for
slippery earth below.*

And the river goes on forgetting.

[ch. two]

I am intrigued by Rosalia, my great-grandmother. Haunted by her, in fact. When I was a young girl in the 1970s, my mom worked at the Credit Union and my dad ran our family's hardware and grocery store. My grandmother, Mom's mom, took care of me after school. Helen (Helen Banton by then, for she'd outlived two husbands) was a foreign creature, quiet and stern, impossibly old. She wore housedresses and black-rimmed glasses. I remember her boiling calves' brains for lunch and pasteurizing milk in a tall pot on the stove. She fixed me grilled cheese sandwiches, taught me how to bake bread, how to knit, and took me to the Lakeview Ladies' quilting bees. I would sit underneath, with all the knees and ankles, and watch the needles come through my multi-coloured canopies. Some nights the two of us would sleep in her double bed. I remember the sounds of her wind-up clock ticking through the night. Her bottle of Rolaids, set beside the bed, loomed large in the amber streetlight. I loved her with all of my eight-year-old heart.

Later, after a university degree, I decided to spend a summer at home before moving away to graduate school in Ontario. It was clear that Grandma, now living in a small seniors' home with her television and her budgie, wasn't long for the world. She was losing weight. There was hushed talk of cancer. Her newly apparent mortality and my imminent departure from Alberta made me realize how little I knew about her. I began to drop by her place in the afternoons with a tape recorder.

Like any novice historian, I had hoped for a clean narrative with a beginning, middle, and end. Instead, my grandmother's stories were an odd assortment of moments, offered up in no particular order, and without a hint of their importance. Her father had worked in the Hillcrest mine in the Crowsnest Pass while the family lived across the tracks in Bellevue, in a house built from logs he had cut with a broad axe. She remembered him shingling the roof, and chinking cement between the logs to stop the draughts. The walls inside were plastered, and under the plank floor was a space for storing vegetables. A neighbour had made them a door of heavy canvas set within a wooden frame and painted over with beautiful designs. Her mother and father shared a bed on one side of the single bedroom; a second bed on the other side held all of the kids. An uncle slept on a cot in the living room. It was warm up in the mountains, my grandmother told me, but when the snow fell it could cover the windows. One neighbour couldn't open her door when it snowed; she had the kids use a chamber pot and threw the contents out the window.

After Hillcrest, they moved north to a place called Mountain Park, and my grandmother was sent to school with the Grey Nuns in St. Albert, near Edmonton. The girls stayed on one side of the fence, the boys on the other. They went to church every morning before school. There were Indian kids in the school, and while white kids were given a proper MacIntosh apple every day, Grandma said, Indian kids were given only crab apples. Everyone was quarantined in 1918 because of the Spanish flu. Sometimes a mother would come to visit her child but not be allowed in; she would sit on the porch and speak through a window. Grandma's little sister, Annie, caught the dreaded virus and became very ill but recovered. Grandma stayed in the convent for one year, until her parents decided to try out a homestead in Delburne. The prairie was so different from the mountains, she told me. You could see for miles around and everything was so flat, so windy. Her little brother Tom believed the trees created the wind and once declared he would cut down all the wind.

Marriage and kids came eventually, along with cream to sell, houses to clean, a team of horses to drive for the community school. Those later days she didn't remember so well. I don't think she liked getting old.

That summer Grandma and I drank gallons of Earl Grey tea with tiny spoons of sugar while she doled out her stories. The next time I saw her, when I walked into her hospital room back home in Elnora after a long flight from Kingston, I recoiled at the tiny pale body gasping for air, my mother ragged in a chair beside her. Grandma was gone in a few days. Our summer together remains precious to me.

As my grandmother has settled into my own history, it has slowly occurred to me that she not only belongs to me but to another history: the history of women who came to the west with nothing but faith and strong backs and created their own meaning from soil and sky. Grandma gave me her particular meaning, and I've modified it with my own faith and strong back. I, too, am part of that history, I have come to want to find its source. That source, for me, is Rosalia.

Who was she? Why did she come? Grandma told me the coal camps were a "rough and ready" place for a child to grow up. What about for the women raising those children, drawn (or hurled) from every which direction into the rocky jumble at the base of Crowsnest Mountain? What did they leave behind in their home countries? What did they bring with them? What was it like to watch their only connection to the New World leave every morning to walk into a dark mine?

I once made my living as a journalist. Journalists know the present is a shifty thing, but often — wrongly — take the past as knowable. Trying to retrace the steps of my great-grandmother and so many women like her may be a folly. Perhaps that is why it is so appealing.

[ii]

The train west takes twelve days and thirteen
hours. She watches hills swell and dip like waves.
She watches limestone bluffs rush the tracks and
stop cold. Mornings, she wakes to yet more forest
and wonders if the train has moved at all. In
Manitoba, fields of grass appear deep enough
to drown a child. Westward, the grass shrinks,
as though singed by the sun.

So much wood, so little history, the paint in
all the land still wet. The train rocks on and on.

Those who brave the wilderness carve it into
their own likeness.

[ch. three]

First step: start with the specifics and move out from there.

My search for Rosalia begins with a page from a book about the history of Delburne, Alberta. It's called *Through the Years*, and is one of the many dozens of such books Albertans produced about themselves around the time of the seventy-fifth anniversary of the province. The entry for the Andrew Zak family was written by his daughter Annie. It tells me that Rosalia's last name was Patala, that she married Andrew Zak in 1904 in a place called Michelle, BC, and shortly after contracted rheumatic fever and spent months in bed. Their first child was born a year after their marriage, and was dead within the month.

This is all I know of Rosalia's early life, so I set out to investigate, beginning with what remains of my family's living memory of Andrew and Rosalia. I write to all of her grandchildren about my project. While I wait to hear back, I search Calgary's superlative Glenbow Archives online and find nothing about my family. I realize I need to make a trip to the archives in person, in order to get a fuller picture of life in the coalmine towns.

My first pass at an oral family history yields very little. Mom tells me Rosalia's uncle, the man who worked with Andrew, may have been someone called Tony Trstensky. Working down the generations, I contact a cousin in Toronto whom I have never met; Lucinda picked up the phone one Friday night and said she's been to Ellis Island in New York and seen Rosalia's immigration record there. This should at least give me her place of origin. I find the records online and try the search myself, looking for an "R. Patala" who arrived prior to 1904.

Nothing.

I try a dozen different spellings and find a Rosalia Padale who arrived from Valledolmo at the age of forty-three, a forty-six-year-old Rosalia Patella who arrived from Corleone, and a Rosaria Pedala from S. Agala, who came at the age of thirty-three. These women were all too old, according to the family lore. A Rozalia

Patalen arrived from Lelesz, but she was only fifteen. Rosa Patella, an Italian, came from Vallata at an unknown age aboard the *Tartar Prince* from Naples. And the Hungarian Rosalia Patla was eighteen when she arrived on August 22, 1902, aboard the *Columbia*, having departed from an unknown port. Slovakia was part of the Austro-Hungarian Empire at this time, so it's possible my great-grandmother could have been listed as Hungarian. But I can't be sure that this is her record, and even if it is, it doesn't list her place of residence. Perhaps she was never recorded, perhaps she stowed away. Anything is possible.

So many women with their bags and betrothals.

I decide to leave Rosalia for the time being and begin searching the records for Andrew Zak (and Ziak, which Lucinda says means "scholar" in Slovak, from which Zak may have been shortened) and Tony Trstensky, but also with no luck. On the Internet I find a reference to a book called *Crowsnest and Its People.* There is an entry for Henry Zak Sr., but no mention of an Andrew.

I really haven't a clue how to go about tracking people who are long dead, but records of family events such as marriage, births, and deaths seem to be a good place to start. The Delburne history book says they were married in Michelle, BC. I search for a place called Michelle, BC, and can't find it, which makes me doubt anew everything I'd read in the family history. I contact Alberta Vital Statistics and send in a request for a marriage registration for Andrew Zak and Rosalia Patala in the Crowsnest Pass three years on either side of January 1, 1904. Nothing. When I call, they suggest I contact the Alberta Provincial Archives. Nothing there either.

At this point I have only Annie's account of Andrew and Rosalia's life, none of which I've been able to confirm. I decide I won't be able to find these things on the other end of my Internet connection in Newfoundland, and begin to plan a trip back to Alberta.

[iii]

Three years before this, when the world over-
flowed with daughters, she packed her hopes in
a steamer trunk and took a horse-drawn cart to
Hamburg. She held her breath for six long days
and nights as the ship took her west and west,
until she feared she'd never see land again.

Today she arrives on the platform in shiny shoes
and a coat red as a poppy. A small man is here to
meet her. He is missing a finger and smells faintly
of breakfast. Her babies wait in his belly, but first
there will be a house to build and weather to learn.

There are no words for this except Yes.

[ch. four]

After three hours of sleep and nine hours on planes, I land in Calgary at noon on a Tuesday in February, five degrees under a cornflower-blue sky. I collect my bags and make for downtown, where I will drop my things at a hotel and head to the Glenbow Archives — to look for what, I'm not yet sure.

I watch out the bus window. From twenty-six thousand feet in the air the land was white, but down here on the ground the grey-blonde stubble of spring reveals itself. A mapgie. A sagging barn. The city so close to what was recently farm. Two years of drought have scorched the grass along the roads to a nearly featureless mulch, as though green were an idea best left unspoken in polite society.

The woman at the Glenbow Archives is tall, with short curled hair, clear blue eyes and saintly patience. She doesn't even laugh when I tell her I'm writing a book. She warns me that the files will be dirty, and that I might want to wear gloves: after all, the ledgers have come from a coal mine. She disappears with the little slip of paper that bears my scribbled request.

A search of the records has already told me neither Rosalia nor Andrew made it into the official history of the Crowsnest Pass: no union positions, no police records, no photos, no mention in the papers. I decide to try to fill the holes in what I've already learned. Perhaps later, with my family, I'll be able to extract some stories or find some dusty box of documents that everyone now assures me does not exist. I decide to limit my search to before 1918, when I know they left the Pass for mines to the north. I search for diaries written by Crowsnest women. There is nothing of the sort. I read annual reports of West Canadian Collieries, Ltd., peruse labour contracts with the United Mine Workers of America, and thumb my way through cost ledgers for monies spent and received by the company in its town-sites. I even roll out blueprints to get a sense of what the prominent buildings were like inside. I overwork the photocopier into a lather.

I never quite give up hope that on some forgotten page of a company record there will be a reference to Andrew — an accident at work, a paycheque entry, the balance of rent owed on a property. The item that I am now waiting for I have saved for last. The archivist wheels out a large book on a trolley, much as one might a corpse. A pair of clean white cotton gloves lies folded on top.

The Employee Registry for West Canadian Collieries, 1907–1915, is the size of a small tabletop and must weigh as much as a brick of cattle salt. Its cover is mud-coloured leather over hardboard with blood-red corners; its end papers are mottled plum and sand, and bear ripples like a geological map with veins of gold throughout. It is, as I have been warned, dirty. I bend to smell the pages: no coal left, just age. This is the moment I am sure I will see my great-grandfather's name penned in the company ledger, in the studied cursive of the time, when he was still young and none of us had yet happened. Here he stands before me, before the clerk, the waist of his trousers loosely suspended above his hips by a pair of abused blue braces. His face is not yet leathered by the prairie sun. He holds his cap as he provides the company with his next of kin and sole dependent: Wife.

But no. Scores of names, many of them illegible. Andrew Zak is not among them.

It seems the man was never born, never married, never worked for WCC Ltd., never ran for office, never had a run-in with the law, never spoke to a reporter or penned a letter, never longed for the sun in the morose, dripping darkness of the mine. And yet he must have. But if I'm having this much trouble uncovering anything about a man who worked for a powerful, profitable mining company, how will I ever find out anything about his wife?

My first day at the archives closes with a thud and I retire to my hotel to read through my reams of photocopies.

Some time in the night I chuckle at my own stupidity. My grandmother told me she lived in Bellevue but that her father worked in the Hillcrest mine. Hillcrest wasn't owned by WCC Ltd., it was owned by the Hillcrest Coal & Coke Company. There's hope yet.

The next morning I wander down Stephen Avenue to the Glenbow, sign in at the front desk, take the elevator to the sixth floor, and locate the Hillcrest records. Out comes a trolley of microfilm canisters in tattered cardboard boxes labelled in a kind of well-intentioned anarchy. The man at the desk shows me how to load the microfiche reader and leaves me to it.

The names listed, the small fraction that are legible, are neither alphabetical nor chronological. With growing impatience, I load and unload each of the dozen or so boxes. The earliest records I can find are from 1922, four years after Andrew left the Pass.

I push the trolley back to the desk and flip through my note-book looking for a few last items to search. I decide to try a few more union records before calling it a wrap. I send the ever-patient archivist another scrap of paper and find a spot at a table next to two people who've been researching past owners of a piece of contested land. The archivist emerges with the books, smiles and returns to her black computer monitor.

And there he is!

In a foolscap-sized, hand-bound book of army-fatigue canvas and rust-coloured leather there is a subscription list for the UMWA's newsletter, The District Ledger: Andrew Zak, membership begun August 30, 1918, and charged to the Yellowhead Coal Company. Another entry on the same date lists his address as Coalspur, and a third lists it care of C. Coal Company, Cadomin.

I stare at the pages. I look away, then back, expecting the entries to have disappeared as the hallucinations they surely must be. But there he is: Andrew Zak. A young man with a young family, and nearly twenty years already worked in the mines, who, eighty years from now, will have a great-granddaughter who will fly in a jet from the western shores of the Atlantic Ocean with a computer smaller than a placemat to look for shreds of his life. I feel overwhelming relief at having found this one small toehold for my family's lore. It's possible this story of Rosalia is true. I want to tell the couple beside me, show them the proof, like pictures of a new baby.

Coalspur and Cadomin are not in the Crowsnest Pass. These places represent the family's last years in the mines, along what was known as the Coal Branch up near Jasper. They're not the years I was looking for, but it's just like Grandma said. The rest must be at least partly true.

[iv]

A wolf howls out of loneliness, not rage, but

listening from behind flimsy frontier timbers,

she can't tell. That, and the chorus of whiskey on

the street outside her window — bottles and voices

and the odd wet thud — is the first night of the

rest to come.

    She lies awake, held hostage.

[ch. five]

Next morning, I check out of my hotel and pick up a car at a rental agency around the corner. I ask for advice on driving the mountain roads at this time of year, and find my way to Highway 22X, bound for the Pass. I'm to call Caron Townsend once I'm there. Her name came to me early in my research, when I called the municipal offices of the Crowsnest Pass to ask for the names of local women who have an interest in history. I've told her to expect me around noon.

In the years I've been away I've come to enjoy driving the highways of southern Alberta in a borrowed car almost more than anything. My old need to run away from here, to prove (to myself) that there is a larger world beyond, has quieted. Now the big blue sky and the vast distances are a comfort. Wallace Stegner said that on the prairies a man is an exclamation point: a solitary thing. In the years I have spent living in cities far from the open fields I think of as home, I have yearned for this. Today the snow is patterned with the path of animals and there is a misty light coming through the high, high clouds. The trees of the foothills are black as coal. Hawks sit on power poles in their heavy cloaks and clouds advance over the mountains from the west, rolled like knuckles. I should know what this means, I should be able to read the weather, but I can't. It's hard to imagine this place a century ago, without contrails and fences, wires and asphalt.

Just before noon I pull into Blairmore and step out into the crisp mountain air. The wind is blowing (as usual) and the sun is in my eyes (as usual). I run into a gas station to call Caron: she tells me to meet her down the road at a restaurant in Coleman, Popiel's Family Restaurant, for a bite to eat. I arrive before her and sit out front on a small patch of grass. A few minutes later she pulls up in her blue Oldsmobile and unloads a paper grocery bag big enough to hold a small goat.

Inside, we pick a table a little out of the way, order tea, and she shows me the contents of the bag: three books about the history of the Crowsnest Pass, totalling something like fifteen hundred pages,

I guess, including *Crowsnest and Its People*, the book I had found online: pay dirt.

We talk about life in the Pass and she answers my questions candidly. She has spent her life in the Pass, has just retired from forty years of nursing, and is a volunteer at the local museum. I tell her that I want to meet the oldest women in the community, to get a sense of what life must have been like for my grandmother and her contemporaries. She says she knows just the person, but we should eat first, then drop in on Mrs. Fontana unannounced, because if given the time to say no, she just might.

We pull up in front of a 1940s-style one-storey house and go to the back, let ourselves through the gate, and knock on the door. We wait for a few moments, and when no one answers, Caron opens the door and calls out.

A high-pitched woman's voice and the barking of an excited dog come in reply. We step into the back porch and Veronica Fontana comes toward us through her kitchen, apologizing for a mess I hadn't noticed. Like so many others in town, her basement has just flooded and she has brought up all her things — plastic containers of sewing supplies, flats of canned and boxed food.

Veronica is wearing a flowered T-shirt and long skirt. Her white hair is thinning and her eyes are alert and blue. Behind her on the dark panelled wall hangs a framed picture of the Virgin Mary. Hunkering at her feet is a growling, yapping youngster of a mutt. Veronica takes my hand and holds it in hers while Caron introduces me and my business. Veronica says she is glad to know me and leads us through the kitchen to the living room. She shows us the new shoes she has just bought but will be forced to return — they surely weren't wide enough for her swollen feet. She raises her long skirt to show us. It's a shame, she says, the blue wedge-heeled mules would have been a nice change from her sneakers. She fusses with mending scattered over the couch and clears a place for us to sit. She flops back in her recliner like a Rembrandt in the yellow light of her gauzy curtains and asks us what we want to know. I tell her. Without hesitation, Veronica begins with her father.

"My dad, he came from the old country when they had that upris-ing in Czechoslovakia, eh? My mother's parents, they turned around and they fled to Budapest. And from Budapest — they never had no education or nothing — they put them on the boat to go to New York. My mother was only twelve years old when they shipped her over, and she couldn't read or write. She met my dad down there, and they were married when they were about sixteen and eighteen. Well, his brother kept calling him to come over, so he came to Can-ada and went to work up at Lille. I was born in Blairmore in 'twenty-two. And from there, well, then it was the hungry thirties."

Veronica must have been about ten years younger than my grand-mother. I encouraged her to tell me as much as she could remember about what things were like in her mother's — and Rosalia's — time.

"Well, we were lucky. My father and mother, they had a big gar-den. We had two big lots, they were seventy-five by one hundred [feet], and we had the house right in the middle there. One part of the thing was potatoes. Half of another one was cabbages, and then peas and carrots and turnip, horse beans, beets, and parsnip. We lived on vegetables. We had a few chickens. I used to go out and sell the eggs for five cents a dozen, and that's how we used to pay our bill at Thompson's, by bringing eggs to the store, and they used to deduct them. You could buy a great big basket of cherries for two bits. A loaf of bread was ten cents. And we had a cow. People used to laugh at all the Slovaks that used to eat the cottage cheese, eh? Sour milk and cottage cheese. Sour milk was really good with mashed potatoes. But we were brought up on that. We crave it every now and then. And you figure, a family of eight, my mother used to make great big pots of mashed potatoes and put caraway seed in. I remember her with one of these big basins, and she used to make bread a couple of times a week. Well, you take trying to feed eight, that was something, eh? And the priest used to preach, 'Raise the family, raise kids! Don't let the nickel squeal in your pocket.' That's why I never bothered much with church."

Her memory is better than mine, despite her age. I can't believe my luck.

"My father built our house with the logs he used to bring down from the hill. There was no nails. The logs were dovetailed. They used to get the moss and fill them in, and then there was wallboard. We had electricity, one light in each room. My father put in a sink and a water tap. There was five rooms. There was three beds in the one bedroom, and the girls stayed in there. My brothers slept on the couch in the other.

"Women used to deliver their babies on their own, believe it or not. And that's why Mother lost the twins, because there was no medical thing going at all. And when all the epidemics used to go around, there was polio, scarlet fever, and everybody used to be quarantined that had it. You had a great big sign on your fence. Everybody had to stay on their own property; you couldn't go anywhere because the disease spread so fast. A truant officer used to go around checking to make sure you didn't go out of your yard."

I ask her about family traditions. She cocks her head and looks out the corner of her bold blue eyes.

"Christmas was good. We'd have chicken, and Father used to buy a ham. Of course, ham was cheap at that time. They used to sell the meat, anybody who had a pig or something like that, they'd sell the meat for ten cents a pound. You figure, when you paid five cents a dozen for eggs, eh? That went a long ways. And Mother used to make some kind of plum pudding with rice. We had mashed potatoes, and we had our own peas. It wasn't luxury, but there was food on the table all the time. But you know what we had for decorations on the tree? We used to put silver on walnuts and things like that. Silver paper from the cigarette packages. And that's the way our tree was decorated. Then we'd find old tubes from tires, and we used to cut doll shapes out of that, and out of the catalogue. We'd cut out all the [pictures of] bedding and the beds, and we used to take cardboard boxes and make rooms and put all these different things in them. That was our game. Our doll house. There was no such a thing as anything to go under the tree."

I ask if her mother ever talked about being unhappy.

"No. Well, they were so busy, they had lots of work to do and everything else. They used to have the flour in 100-pound sacks. And my mother used to make us our dresses and pants out of them. And the sugar sacks. Then when the cement plant closed down, holy cow, there was so many of these cement bags there, everybody down our street used to get them and make sheets and pillow cases, whatever you needed for dish cloths and that."

At the end of an hour, the restless dog has long since fallen asleep at her feet. Though Veronica shows no signs of tiring, it's time for Caron and I to go. I turn off my recorder and thank Veronica for taking the time to talk to a stranger.

The Crowsnest Museum occupies two storeys of an old school house just up the street from where an old garage was once turned into a movie set, and across the way from a now-empty newspaper building. The guestbook shows there's not much in the way of visitor traffic in the month of February. Caron and Operations Manager Wendy Zack (no relation, as it happens) show me through the half-dozen rooms, through boxes of mining equipment (a safety lamp, a canary cage, a harness for a mine pony), through cordoned-off demonstration rooms of a house (an Eaton's cupboard, an oval copper laundry kettle, a handmade cradle), a display of three wedding dresses and a buffalo-hide jacket, a glass cabinet of trophies and sports jackets, a camera collection and a fiddle belonging to one Mr. Gushul, an old player piano.

Back in Wendy's office — a desk behind a partition in the gift shop — I tell her a bit about my project, my family's connection to the Pass, and my difficulties trying to find records of Andrew and Rosalia. I tell her about finding a listing for Henry Zak in the first edition of *Crowsnest and Its People*, but that I'd never heard of him and wasn't sure if he was related. Wendy listens patiently, then pulls out her own tattered copy of the book and flips to the back. She opens the book to a photo of Henry Sr. He is standing proudly at the counter of his butcher shop. The image could have been taken yesterday, but of my cousin David: the same nose, the same cheeks.

But nowhere in the family history is a mention of Andrew. What is this refusal by official history to release anything about him, or about his wife, whom I am increasingly obsessed with knowing, or about their lives together in this place? Why is it as if they never existed? How many people like them helped make this country, but were never recorded?

Historical despair being an occupational hazard in her line of work, Wendy nods and walks to a glassed-in book cabinet across the room. She pulls out a binder and flips to the birth registries, to the section on Passburg, now a kind of suburb of Bellevue.

And there, in the hand-scrawled ledger, is a listing for Thomas Joseph Zak, male, born to Andrew Zak in Maple Leaf on November 18, 1914.

Thomas Zak. Tom. Uncle Tom. Grandma's kid brother, the one with the peculiar theory about wind.

I am pleased. Another toehold — and a second source — for the story, to be sure. But what about the others? Why are they so invisible?

I take a photocopy for Aunt Cec, Uncle Tom's widow. I buy a copy of the second edition of *Crowsnest and Its People*. This one has all new information, Wendy assures me, and the first one is out of print. Caron shows me out and I tell her I hope to be back in the summer.

Driving to my parents' home in central Alberta, my mind goes blank to the rumble of the tires and the gentle mumbling of the radio. I wonder how I'm going to write a story which has so many holes, and just why the holes are so compelling. The wide road is empty on this long Friday night. While I don't yet know what Andrew and Rosalia came to, perhaps it is time to try to understand what they left.

[v]

There is a wedding. Which is to say, a bath,
a dress with whalebone stays, a garland of
rosemary about the waist, a visit to the priest,
a kiss — vertigo, vertigo — signatures, a ring
that will do, a meal with wine.

And then.

An unfamiliar hand with not enough fingers,
hard as a spade but kind. Trembling, even. A
candle giggling at the bedside. Lips and salt on
the tongue, the noisy mind tucked neatly away
in the cupboard.

The world tilting, ever so slightly.

[ch. six]

There isn't a whole lot of Slovakian history available to the average writer in Newfoundland. All I know is that the Fontanas and the Zaks were only two families among an army of Slovaks who came to the New World in the early years of the twentieth century. In the early nineteen hundreds, thirty thousand people left what is now present-day Slovakia every year. Having lost one-third of its population, Slovakia ties with Ireland for Europe's highest rate of emigration. Like the Irish, the Slovaks fled poverty and oppression. But unlike the Irish, the Slovaks have not created an internationally accessible canon of literature and art to capture their stories. Does this help explain why my own family never bothered to keep records of its own early history in Canada? Did they think the story not worth telling? That no one would be interested?

Fortunately, my cousin Lucinda took pity on me and sent me a book, *A History of Slovakia*, written by Stanislav Kirschbaum of York University in Toronto. I'm not sure what it can tell me about Rosalia, but it is all I have to go on. It tells the story of a people struggling for their identity and their survival.

I learn that the land below the Tatra Mountains (northern Slovakia) was settled by the Slavs, the ancestors of today's Slovaks, in the sixth century. Emperor Charlemagne and the Franks began making inroads into present-day Slovakia in the eighth century. By the ninth century, the rulers of two Slavic principalities, Morava and Nitra, had asked for missionaries from Constantinople (then capital of the Byzantine Empire, also known as the Eastern Roman Empire) to help them resist the influence of the Frankish clergy. The brothers Constantine (Cyril) and Methodius, who knew the language of southern Slavs, accepted the invitation to Christianize the Slavs, invented a new alphabet for all Slavs called Glagolitic, and then went on to use it in their translations of the liturgy. Slovaks now regard the brothers' arrival as the crowning achievement of "Great Moravia," the state that was formed when the two principalities were united under one ruler; in addition, their own language was granted authority by the all-powerful Latin church. However, a new pope who did not approve soon took over and curtailed the use of the Slavonic liturgy. Shortly thereafter, the Magyars — nomadic horsemen, now known as Hungarians — invaded and brought Great Moravia to an end. The Great Moravian period lasted less than seventy-five years, and it was the only time Slovaks would enjoy a state for a millennium. According to Kirschbaum, throughout history, whenever Slovaks sought a common historical thread for their identity they turned to the Cyrillo-Methodian tradition. People in the region never stopped speaking their own language, despite many attempts to obliterate it.

With the Magyar invasion in the tenth century, Slovakia became part of the Kingdom of Hungary. Latin became the official language of the kingdom, and all power lay with the Magyar nobles and the king. Germans were encouraged to settle in mining towns and brought with them their language, arts, and trades. Things stayed this way throughout the rest of the Middle Ages and the Renaissance, while the mining of silver, copper, and gold flourished.

In the sixteenth century, the Ottoman Turks threatened Central Europe. After the last Hungarian king was killed, Hungarian (and neighbouring Bohemian) nobles elected Austrian Duke Ferdinand Habsburg as King, thereby creating the Habsburg Empire — the Catholic Habsburgs were already rulers of Austria and Spain. Magyar refugees (mostly nobles) from Turkish-controlled lands fled to Slovakia. Slovak towns thus became populated with Germans, Magyars, and Slovaks. In fact, in the early seventeenth century, the Hungarian legislative body gave Germans, Magyars, and Slovaks an equal share of municipal power in many towns.

It is also at this time that the Reformation spread throughout Slovakia. The Habsburgs launched the Counter-Reformation from the Slovak town of Trnava, where a Catholic university was created; its press published a hymnal called the *Cantus Catholici*, written in Slovak. This publication testified to the role of the church in keeping the Slovak language alive from the days of Cyril and Methodius, which was considered good for Slovak culture. Their language, however, was still a distant fourth in terms of power. Latin was the language of administration, Magyar was still the language of the Hungarian landowners, and in the cities and towns, German remained the language of the merchant class. Hearing the liturgy in Slovak, while good for the spirit, did not change the fact that Slovaks had no middle class or nobility, and the people remained politically disadvantaged. Peasants were still required to provide so-called *robot* in exchange for their access to farmland, which was payment to landlords in the form of often unspecified amounts of cash, products, and labour. Politics was a play they merely watched; landowners and magnates were the characters. The Turkish occupation of Hungary and the consequences of the Reformation and Counter-Reformation provoked many rebellions in Slovakia, and one of them gave rise to the folk hero Juro Jánosik, a Robin Hood character who was executed in the early eighteenth century at the age of twenty-five and soon immortalized in ballads and songs. There were even many films made about him in Slovakia.

The eighteenth century in Europe saw the birth of baroque art. With its curved lines and elaborate scrollwork, it was associated with the Counter-Reformation and a reinvigorated Catholicism. It was also the time of the Enlightenment, which emphasized the primacy of reason. The century continued with moderate advances in the rights of Slovaks. The Hungarian legislative body passed a new law that, while failing to emancipate Slovakian peasants, at least defined and limited the *robot* to cash plus one-ninth of their products and compulsory labour (52 days with animals, or 104 without). A new village school system was established, where instruction was offered in local languages.

But better times were not to last for Slovaks. Late in the eighteenth century, after the Turks were chased out of Hungary, the Hungarian government began an official policy of assimilating non-Magyars, even though Magyars constituted less than half the population of the kingdom. Famine and cholera killed tens of thousands in eastern Slovak villages. In 1840, the Hungarian legislative body passed a new law that replaced Latin with Magyar as the kingdom's official language; young Slovak intellectuals, led by Ľudovít Štúr, stood their ground by developing a literary language from the central Slovak dialect as a tool to unite all Slovaks.

They also began the *drobná práca* ("menial tasks") movement, including reading circles, temperance clubs, self-help groups, and central Europe's first farmers' union. They eventually formed the Slovak National Council, whose military units attacked the Hungarian army. They failed in their attempt to control Slovakia, but did at least succeed in abolishing the *robot*. Many peasants subsequently sold their land, moved into the towns, and became the pool from which the working class developed. The nationalist intelligentsia, however, failed to stop Magyarization; in addition, the Habsburgs annulled the Hungarian constitution and German was made the official language in the Habsburg Empire. Still, Slovak cultural life was not stifled. Budapest, however, reacted with more aggressive policies. By 1861, no Slovak-only schools were left, and although there was some teaching in the Slovak language in Catholic secondary schools, it was understood that all members of society above the peasant workers should speak and understand Magyar.

Though relations between Slovaks and Magyars had never been bad, they soon deteriorated because of Magyarization. In 1867, the year of Canada's Confederation, Hungary extracted more power from Austria, and out of this arrangement the Habsburg Empire became the Austro-Hungarian Empire. Over the next several years, large swaths of land were confiscated for Magyars, causing famine among Slovaks. Into this world was born Andrej Hlinka, who became a fabled Slovak politician. Ordained as a Catholic priest, he was well known as a social worker and fiery orator. He joined the Slovak National Party in 1901 and was subsequently suspended from the church, found guilty of "instigation against the Magyar nationality," and sentenced to two years in jail. While serving his time, parishioners of his hometown Černova wanted him to consecrate a church he'd helped build. Ecclesiastical authorities refused, and instead sent Magyar clergy. The parishioners, packed together in a narrow roadway, tried to prevent the clergy from doing their work, and the police fired into the crowd. Fifteen people were killed and more than seventy injured. The event received world-wide attention.

In 1914, the assassination of the heir to the Austro-Hungarian throne, Archduke Franz Ferdinand, sparked a world war, and four years after that, the empire fell, the dynasty's massive holdings scattering into new nations. In 1918, Slovakia became part of Czechoslovakia, where it was to stay until the so-called Velvet Revolution of 1989 and the emergence of the independent Slovak Republic in 1993.

And there it remains. Surrounded by the cultural jewels of Prague and Austria to the west, and by Ukraine to the east and Poland to the north — the motherlands of so many western Canadians — Slovakia seems to the Western eye, in contrast, reclusive and distant.

Not unlike a couple of people I know.

[vi]

In the end — or the beginning — it is his back she
begins to love. More precisely, the way it gives
ever so slightly under her soapy cloth, the barrel
plimmed and the water heated. The bathwater
around him grows greasy with the day that is
always night and the hammers that ping and ping.

There are cracks where the darkness will
always hide.

[ch. seven]

Aunt Cecilia Hučala — she's not really my aunt, but rather some combination of once-removeds and second this or that which I cannot determine — came to Canada from Nižná, Czechoslovakia, with her mother and her little sister in 1938. Cecilia was fourteen years old and hadn't seen her father since she was two; he'd preceded them to seek his fortune, living with his sister near Trochu, Alberta, and taking various jobs on farms, on the railway, and in the mines of the Pass. It was only when the family home in Nižná burned to the ground, leaving them homeless, that Cecilia's mother wrote to her husband and demanded he do something. She arranged their papers, made a bone-chilling trip out of the country (it was the height of World War II, and a German border guard believed they were escaping Jews), and joined him in Alberta, where he left the mines to work out a homestead near Delburne. Ten years later, twenty-four-year-old Cecilia would land a job as a cook in a logging camp where a certain Tom Zak — my grandmother's little brother — was working. Three weeks later, she would sweep him right off his feet and out of a prior wedding engagement. She and Tom married in 1948.

Aunt Cec has a sharp mind — she was rumoured to have known the birthdays of all her children's classmates — as well as a keen interest in politics and history. Her only memory of Rosalia, who died two weeks before Cecilia's wedding to Tom, was of combing the old woman's thinning hair as she lay in a Red Deer hospital bed. Andrew, however, lived with his son and new daughter-in-law for several years after they married. Furthermore, Cecilia and Andrew both spoke Slovak. Aunt Cec's place, therefore, had to be the next stop in my journey. I collect Andrew's oldest living grandchildren, Kay and Johnny (along with his wife Marie, of Czech descent), and together we make the trip to the seniors' home in Stettler where Aunt Cec has recently moved. The four of us buzz ourselves through the double glass doors in the lobby, pass the dining room where staff are setting tables for supper to the blare of a country music station, find our way to the elevator and up to the second floor. Still tall in her eighties, Aunt Cec meets us part of the way down the hall with arms outstretched. She takes my hand and leads us back to her apartment. *Question Period* is on the television and the late afternoon sun teases the curtains of her patio doors. She sits us in chairs and on the sofa; I plunk down on the floor at the foot of her recliner and set up my tape recorder. Talking to Aunt Cec is like riding a bicycle downhill: you get on, hold on, and worry later about the brakes. Her daughter, Lucinda, has already told her what I am after, and she immediately begins answering questions I've not yet asked.

"Mrs. Zak was born in Trstená," she says, taking up a pen and writing out the sentence she'd just spoken in a deliberate, shaky hand. "Grandpa Zak, Kvačany. On the Slovakia side. That's where I was born, in Slovakia."

She says the names again and again, trying to coax the right sounds from my mouth. I'm thrilled that I finally have something to go on from their life before they arrived in Canada. I ask her if she's been to these towns.

"Oh yes, I've been there. Actually, Trstená is under water because they wanted a big dam. The dam goes right into Poland." My heart sinks a little. So much for a pilgrimage there. "He was born more to the east in the mountains. It was only a poor area in the country. At least that's what my mother used to say. She used to say the land had more forest there, it wasn't quite as good.

"They hated Hungarians," she offers, as I struggle to keep up, "because, of course, they bossed them around too much. Mother didn't like Polish people either. I don't know why. They just sort of hated each other, those people. My dad — and he was in the first world war — said, 'There was never peace here, and there never will be.' Which was pretty well true. They had a lot of trouble, see, with the Austro-Hungarians."

"Because Czechoslovakia was a rich country," Johnny adds. "Everyone wanted a piece of it. Or all of it.'"

"A rich country because of coal?" I ask.

"Coal," Johnny confirms, "and I think there's quite a bit of mineral there, too. At that time, you see, coal was a big item. And they must have had iron ore too, because they were always manufacturing something. And this is what Germany wanted when they started their war, to make equipment for their factories."

I had never imagined Rosalia's homeland as an industrial landscape. My own mental pictures of the world a hundred years ago are those I have from Alberta: huge expanses of mixed-grass prairie, Blackfoot women with babies looking guardedly into a studio camera, sod huts with stout Scottish women standing at a scrubbing board, stooks of hay ringed by a few intrepid homesteaders. But these images are from a Canadian past, when weather and soil ruled the world; Europe, meanwhile, knew steel and war. Perhaps this, too, was why they wanted out.

"Aunt Cec," I ask, "can you tell me about before they came over? I've heard that Andrew quit school when he was young to sell glass from a sack on his back."

"Yes, he did. He used to carry it on his back. There was no other way, of course, and he had big blocks, you know? Those big pieces of glass. He must have had a knife or something to cut it with."

Another surprise. I had pictured Bohemian glass trinkets, like the ones I've seen lining shelf upon expensive shelf of tourist shops in Prague. "He sold plate glass?" I ask.

Johnny: "Yeah. For windows."

Me: "On his back?"

Johnny: "He'd buy it, then peddle it wherever he could."

Cec adds, "He used to go to Russia with it on his back. One day when he was travelling in Russia, he had to be very careful. They were saying that the czar was going to go through that place and nobody was supposed to be on the streets. They were afraid the czar would get killed, would get shot." I imagine a young Andrew slipping into an alley to watch the parade of Czar Nicholas and his Alexandra, the sun glinting off the jewels in her dress.

I say he must have learned many languages doing this kind of work.

"Quite a few Slovak people could speak German," Cec agrees, "and some could speak Hungarian, too. But they hated Hungarians."

I ask if that racial tension continued when they were all newcomers together in Canada.

"Up until wartime," says Johnny. "After the war, it subsided. I'll tell you, Monica, when we went to town on a Saturday night," he says, recalling the 1930s, "there'd be a group of Ukrainians talking here in their own language, and nobody could understand them. There's another one, Polish, over there, and they were talking away to beat hell. Then you go inside the old coffee shop and there's the Chinamen talking in their language. And everybody was thinking the other one was talking about them, plotting against them! But after the war, it subsided. It was such a mixture of nationalities, nobody paid any attention. Everybody talked English. A lot of these people that come, they could talk German and Ukrainian and French."

These people, such as his grandmother?

"Grandma would like to let you think she couldn't speak English. But Granddad insisted that they were going to talk English in front of the kids. They had quite a few wrangles about this. Grandma used to give me hell because I couldn't speak Czechoslovakian, and Granddad said, 'Who the hell is he going to talk to if he talks Czech and can't talk English? The trees?'"

"Did you learn any Czech or Slovak?" I ask.

"At one time I couldn't speak anything else. Mother could understand Ukrainian and Hungarian, because when the Molnars* come to the country, and they come to visit you, the four of them got in the corner and would sit there and talk Hungarian. What they didn't know was that Mother could understand what they were saying, and she'd tell us what they were talking about after they left. And most of the time they were talking about you!

"But when I was six years old I went to school and the teacher sent me home so I could learn English. From then on, Mother and

---

* Not their real name.

Father started speaking English in the home. And that's when Granddad got the idea we should be speaking English because we couldn't talk to anybody else except their immediate family."

Marie and Kay are not saying much, deferring to Cec and Johnny. I return to the nineteenth century and ask how old Andrew was when he started selling glass.

"Oh, probably fourteen at the most," Cec says. "See, he was an orphan. His father died when he was two years old. So then it was his grandmother that raised him. He did have brothers. He never told me what their names were, but he used to say how tall they were. He used to talk about his grandmother a lot. They grew plums. But being an orphan, there was nothing to stay for, no promise for him."

"So he quit school when we has fourteen to sell glass?"

"Maybe twelve," Johnny says. "I'm pretty sure Dad said you went to school for six years, then went to work for the mine." Peddling glass was his way of staying out of the mine, then. I ask when he came to Canada. 1901, Cec tells me. He was nineteen. It took an adolescence spent on the road and propaganda from a land of opportunity called Canada to revoke his decision to never work underground.

"Uncle Pete told my sister how he came. He went to the United States. He walked across the hills at first, because we lived close to the Tatra Mountains, and those mountains went all the way to Poland. After that, he went on a buggy. They always had connections. And then from there, I don't know if he would have gone on a train, but he went to a port in Poland, where they would have got on the boat. I don't imagine they would have had the money to pay for their transportation. I think they worked the cattle boats."

"Worked their way over," Johnny agrees. "Lots of them did that."

"And Rosalia? How old was she came to New York?"

"I think she was fairly young because there were many, many girls that were trying to escape, to get away from Slovakia. One of them was Mrs. Hugo. She worked for Jews. All those, even Grandma, worked for Jews who taught them German. They knew how to speak German before they learned how to speak English."

"What made her leave Slovakia?"

"Well, they thought gold was just falling down from the sky."

"Did she come by herself?"

"They were coming by themselves. Mrs. Hugo's sister was only thirteen when she came to Canada. But those parents never gave it a thought. Never cared whether those children got lost or whether they lived. It was terrible." Aunt Cec's language has changed. She's gone from *he* to *they*, from history to conjecture. Would Rosalia have taken the same route out of Slovakia as Andrew, through Poland? Probably Poland, Cec says, she wouldn't be a bit surprised.

Aunt Cec seems to be getting tired. I've been peppering her with my questions for an hour. But I want to ask her one last thing.

"What was Mrs. Zak like?"

"Well," she laughs, as a mildly pained expression passes across her face. How could she possibly sum up a woman she had barely known, dead these fifty years? "Just like any other woman, I would say."

She looks towards the kitchen and makes a clucking sound with her tongue. Her son Kenny had taken her to the supermarket to buy some snacks and she hasn't even put them out, she explains, disappointed with her failing memory. Then she turns back to add one final story.

"She wasn't getting along that well with Granddad, so she took the baby. She went there with the baby to the old country. But after being there for a year, I don't think they wanted her anymore because she didn't have any money."

"She went there with Mother?" Johnny asks.

"Grandma took the baby with her, yes. And she stayed over there for a year."

"That's what Mother always told me," Kay adds, speaking for the first time.

"Is that right?" Johnny asks, picking up a can opener from the coffee table, turning its squeaky crank again and again. "I never did hear that story before."

"Because they did not get along, apparently," Cec says. "Granddad, I think, could be quite stubborn, too. And bossy."

"You found that out, too, did you?" Johnny chuckles.

Aunt Cec leaves our assembled circle and retreats to her small kitchen to prepare a quick feast of grapes, shortbread, diet gingerale, and tiny cheesecakes, muttering all the while about how the seniors' home staff won't let her have any pots and pans, and it sure would be nice to bake some cookies once in a while As she ignores our pleas not to fuss, I discuss Rosalia further with Johnny and Kay: they tell me she was short, stout, that she had rheumatic fever twice — something they suspect left her with a weak heart — that she never knit, but regularly boiled young Tom's white shirts and made sure his collars were starched. She always liked having visitors and was afraid of being alone; she had a habit of sawing logs in the evening to fill the time. Their grandfather, they go on, was an angry man, crippled from working the mines, having lost a couple of fingers and gained a permanently dislocated right shoulder. I take out my copy of Tom's birth certificate and leave it on the table for Aunt Cec.

"He was a hard-working man," says Aunt Kay as we move toward Cec's spread with general chat of the cousins' and grandchildren's various comings of age. "He used to get so upset."

On our way back from Stettler, just outside Delburne, Uncle Johnny suggests we stop in at the graveyard. Rosalia and Andrew are both buried there. He can't remember what's on their headstones — it's been a while — but there might be something useful for me. We pull onto the gravel road just east of town. It's coming close to the end of the day and the sun is low on the horizon. Living for so long now on a foggy island in the North Atlantic, I can't believe I once took the sun for granted. A lone horse stands fetlock deep in snow in the corner of a field. There is nothing but stubble on the horizon.

We stop at the gate. Kay and Marie stay in the car while Johnny and I step out into the snow.

It's crusty, most of it, but sometimes we fall through, up to our knees, and curse the snow in our socks. Johnny can't remember where the graves are, so he heads off in one direction while

I go in another. If you ever need evidence of the short tenure of European settlers on the prairies, just head for a cemetery: only a handful of the markers date back even as far as the early 1900s. We pass the vault where bodies used to be kept for the winter, before the town acquired a machine tough enough to dig through the bedrock ice of an Alberta February. We pass headstones bearing names that are familiar to me. Then, towards the back, on a slope facing the east, appears one white headstone adorned with a simple cross:

Rosalya Zak
b. Sept 1, 1884 d. July 30, 1948

Andrew Zak
b. Oct 6, 1882 d. Aug 5, 1959

Even their shared headstone has little to say.

Beside it is a low granite stone with the name Emma Helen Banton. Grandma. I am a little shocked. Having been with her during her last hours of life, I had decided to go back to my research and classes in Ontario before her funeral, so I'd never seen where her ashes had been interred. Part of me had clung to the image of her still sitting in that chair with a cup of Earl Grey, her budgie bird nattering away in the background. I found myself wishing I hadn't seen her name there on the cold ground, surrounded by sculpted snow. Why is the end so silent?

I now have part of what I'd come to Alberta for: the birthplaces of Rosalia Patala and Andrew Zak. According to Aunt Cec, Rosalia's hometown may be under water, but I should still be able to track down histories of the regions, and perhaps see them for myself. There is no atlas in the house so I hit the Internet and soon find a website featuring Slovakian maps — in Slovak, a language with an unsettling number of letters. I take a stab at navigating the page and soon find not one but two different towns named Kvačany. To my surprise, I also find not one but two towns named Trstená, despite Cec's recollection that it had been flooded. One Kvačany is near the city of Prešov in east-central Slovakia; another is near Dolný Kubín in what appears to be the crest of the Tatra Mountains near the Polish border. One Trstená is on the Danube River, a short hike from the Austrian border in the southwest; the other Trstená is in the Tatra Mountains, just south of the gigantic Orava Lake on the Polish border.

I dial Cec's number and ask if she can remember the locations of the towns. She can't; she seems worn out from my earlier questions, and I feel badly for confronting her with more. But I'm so close. I describe the locations of the four towns on the website and ask her which two seem the most likely. She can't remember, maybe another time. I apologize and wish her goodnight.

I look at the map again. She had said they were both in the mountains. She also said Trstená was under water, under a lake created by a hydroelectric dam. Orava Lake? Back to the Internet. On a tourism website for the Orava region (this time in English), I learn that Orava is a man-made lake; construction of the dam began in 1948, and by the time its basin filled in 1953, five towns had been flooded. Trstená, a market town founded in the fourteenth century, was not among them.

I look back at my map and mark the most likely locations of Rosalia and Andrew's hometowns. They are a few miles apart.

The morning before I am to leave for the airport, I feel happy to have the information from Aunt Cec but know I would be much more comfortable if I had even one official document to back up her memories from long ago.

I decide to try one more search.

My attempts to find records of my family through the Alberta government have failed, but in the reading I have been doing of the history of the Crowsnest Pass, and with my recent trip there, it has occurred to me that the interprovincial border might not have meant much to the people who lived there, back when everything was new. Perhaps there are records of the Zaks in British Columbia. The entry in the Delburne history book suggested they were married in the seemingly fictitious town of Michelle. Perhaps there was something to that.

I find a website for the BC Provincial Archive and am happy to see its records are not only abundant, but digitized and searchable. I type in "Zak" and hold my breath.

There are no births and no marriages, but under deaths there are eleven entries. The first one: Helen Zak, died August 27, 1906, age 0, in Michel. Of course: Michel, not Michelle. Michel, a community where every building save for the hotel had been bulldozed in 1967.

Helen was the first baby, who, according to the Delburne history book, died after three weeks. She bequeathed her name to the next baby, my grandmother, Emma Helen. Grandma had always believed she was a twin, and swore that on Rosalia's deathbed her mother had begged her never to look for her birth certificate. What confusions had grown here over the years?

The online index lists only limited information so I call the archives and order the official Death Genealogy Certificate, which, if I'm lucky, will list the birthplaces of the parents of the deceased. The woman on the phone apologizes as she takes my credit card number, explaining that it's a bit of a long shot and I won't know for two to three weeks.

[vii]

Who could know the way a mountain disappears?
The walls have thinned with the fury of her wiping,
the furniture flinches at the sight of her. Every
day, dust in the butter, dust in her underclothes.
Dust like so many blackbirds baked in a pie. Her
dreams are black with it.

Dust like penance.

[ch. eight]

Back in Newfoundland one rainy day, I come home for lunch to find a large manila envelope from BC Vital Statistics drooping wetly over the side of my rusty mailbox. I take off my shoes and coat, lay the envelope on the kitchen table and put the kettle on to boil, all before I can screw up the courage to open the package.

With tea in hand, I unseal the envelope. I skip to the bottom of the page of baby Helen's death certificate:

> Parents – Mother: NOT RECORDED
> Birthplace: NOT RECORDED
> – Father: NOT RECORDED
> Birthplace: NOT RECORDED

Surely, I must have done something terrible in a former life to deserve this. I have my lunch and mope back to work.

But there was another relative I hadn't yet enlisted: Ken Zak, Cec's son and Lucinda's brother. I call him up one day, explain what I am doing, and ask if I can send him the transcript of my interview with Aunt Cec. Would he check it to see if anything in there was not quite right? Could he think of anything to add? He says that would be fine and I email it to him at once.

I contact him again in a couple of weeks.

"The bulk of the information as I read it appears to be correct," his email reads. Then comes the bad news: "Last fall we ran out of room ... and I burned two trunks full of mouse-chewed letters, documents, and tax returns from 1919 on."

I have started to develop a thick skin about this kind of thing, so manage to shrug it off. But then, a few hours later, another email:

Hey Monica,
I shot my mouth a little too soon about the papers. I did save two boxes. Depending on your Slovak, there may be letters of interest to you. Stop over and we can have a digfest.
Ken.

Looks like another trip home for me.

One day, out of spite more than anything, I decide to try searching "Patala" in the BC records. Imagine my surprise upon finding this:

> Groom Name: Andrew Tak
> Place: Michel
> Bride Name: Rosie Patala
> Date: 1905 8 21
> Event: Marriage

Andrew Tak? I guess I can be forgiven for not finding that one. Again, I order the whole document. It arrives in a few long days, and it is nearly illegible. But upon closer inspection I see that Trstená is not an impossible solution to the faint hint of writing on the line for bride's place of birth. Trstená, then, must be the right place. Its appearance on her marriage certificate, plus Cec's description of what must be Orava Lake, is enough for me, and surely as much as I can hope to get.

It occurs to me that with the additional information I've now found, I might be able to go back and sort through the Ellis Island records again to find her.

Rosalia Patla. A Hungarian who arrived in New York at the age of eighteen in 1902 aboard the brand new steamship the *Columbia*, along with 1,300 others, from Hamburg, Germany. My great-grandmother's headstone indicates she was born on September 1, 1884; her marriage certificate indicates she was married in August 1905 at the age of twenty. Patala could easily have been recorded as "Patla," particularly if, when spoken, the emphasis was placed on the first syllable: PA-ta-la. The place of residence on her passenger record is blank so this is no help. But the rest all fits.

This must be her. After a year of looking, I've found her. Now I can begin to quilt together the tiny pieces of her life in the Pass.

When Rosalia emigrated to New York in 1902, having crossed

the Atlantic by herself at the age of eighteen, her future husband had likely already been in the Pass for a year or more. At some point Andrew wrote to her, and some time after that she got on a train, which — according to one family account in *The Crowsnest and its People* of a similar journey — was likely a two-week journey which took her first to Montréal, then to somewhere in the Pass. They married on August 21, 1905 in Michel, BC, just as Alberta was joining Canada. There were already mines in Frank, Lille, Bellevue, Blairmore, and Coleman. On August 27, 1906, twelve months after they married, Rosalia gave birth to baby Helen. Three weeks later she buried her, also in Michel. Soon after, during the worst winter in living memory, she conceived Emma Helen, the first of her four surviving children, who was born on November 5, 1907. Before she was thirty-four, Rosalia had given birth to her four living children in the coal camps of the Rocky Mountains.

There are so many holes in this history. How long was Rosalia in the Pass before they married? Did she accept Andrew's proposal of marriage before she left for the Pass or after she arrived? Did they court? How long did they live in BC? Where did they live before moving to Bellevue? When did they move to Bellevue? Did she really travel home to Trstená with the baby, fed up with life in the Pass? How could she have possibly afforded the journey? Was that baby my grandmother?

So many questions remain. One thing is certain, though: the first two years of her marriage, with the loss of her first child and her entrance into motherhood, must have profoundly changed the young Rosalia.

[viii]

*Meanwhile, her red coat waits with the patience of
houseplants. No operas, no restaurants, only sirens
and wolves and the clomp of boots on the steps. Not
a breath of air in all the blameless weeks.*

*She watches it from time to time, when the spirit
leaves her.*

[ch. nine]

It's July now and I'm on another plane for Alberta, after another last-minute packing job and bleary-eyed drive to the airport for another barely planned research trip to the Crowsnest Pass. This time it's for a reunion of families from Bellevue, Hillcrest, and Passburg. I use my time on the plane to read over what I've compiled so far and try to figure out what I might ask people over the coming weekend of I-don't-know-what. A strange way to do business, really.

A four-year-old girl named Alie sits in the middle seat beside me. She and her mom are Newfoundlanders flying to Fort McMurray to visit Alie's dad. Alie's mom points out something that looks eerily like smoke rising out of the baggage compartment across from us. I turn my head to look and feel a wee hand creeping up the nape of my neck.

I turn back and smile at the little girl, who is kneeling on her seat and looking straight at me. "You have long hair too," I offer.

"My hair's orange. What's yours?"

The colour of dead grass, I want to tell her, but I'm not sure if she'll understand. "Oh, kind of yellow and kind of brown and kind of grey." Alie's mom apologizes and pulls out a paper bag of sweets to offer to her daughter.

A woman traversing a continent to be with her husband who's left home for a high-paying job in the west: I encounter Rosalia everywhere I turn.

My first stop this time will be Vulcan. The old International Hotel from Frank was dismantled and moved there after the Turtle Mountain slide that destroyed much of the town. From the pictures I've seen in the Glenbow Archives, it was stately. I don't know if it would have been representative of hotels of its time — nor do I know if Rosalia and Andrew ever stepped foot in it — but I couldn't pass up the chance to see a real, turn-of-the-twentieth-century Crowsnest Pass hotel. I begin my regular research trip routine, picking up a rental vehicle and heading off south down Deerfoot Trail.

Maybe it's the nine hours on a plane (and it's only noon), or maybe it's my nervousness at the gaping unknown into which I'm about to launch myself (a Pavlovian response after so many years of writing up against deadlines while working as a reporter), but no matter how hard I try, I am unable to think clearly. The suv I'm driving is too new and too big (the rental company didn't have the compact car I'd reserved). There are too many signs for "New Communities," too many identical houses against the stark, blue sky, white with heat, too many construction workers swarming over the latest overpass. I turn on the afternoon thrash show from cjsw, where I got my start in radio fourteen years ago.

Waves of heat make the horizon swim. I think I'll wait for High River before I attempt to think again.

Drive an hour south from Calgary until you hit Highway 23, take a brief detour for dried fruit and an ice cream cone from the restaurant chain where you used to go as a kid, then head east and a bit further south, and you'll come to Vulcan. It's your standard-fare prairie town: slow, wide streets, angle parking with no meters (how civilized this seems), false-fronted stores. In a town like this, time seems to slow the moment you turn down Main Street.

The Vulcan Hotel is a three-storey building, stuccoed like so many others on the prairies just after World War II. There are shiny black bars on the windows. There are two doors, one for the lobby, which looks empty through the glass, and one for the universal Chinese & Western Food Café with its roster of dusty, weathered men pushing greasy concoctions of egg around on their plates. The woman behind the counter doesn't know if this is the hotel I'm talking about and suggests I try somewhere else. But as I thank her and turn to leave, a blonde-haired man on the other side of the restaurant calls me back. He'd overheard my question.

"You looking for the hotel that was in Frank?" he asks, replacing a floppy bucket hat on his dirty head and leaning back in his chair — a highway worker, I figure. "This is it. They moved it over in two parts some time, I don't know when. You need to ask Tina, she's got all the pictures and everything. Go into the bar and ask when she's working. She might be there now. She's got long, brown curly hair." As a backup, he reaches for the cellphone in his pocket and scrolls through for Tina's number.

I look around the restaurant. This is the famed Imperial Hotel from Frank? It's amazing the effect a bit of plywood, some panel board and a few faded colour calendars can have on a place. It's hard to imagine the original.

The lounge is home to a couple of pool tables, a yammering big-screen TV, and a regiment of VLTs. The pictures in the Glenbow showed an ornate carved bar and swinging globe light fixtures, none of which is here now. Once my eyes adjust to the mid-afternoon darkness, I see several tables of men and women parked behind their long-necked beer bottles, with little piles of bills and change sitting at their left hands, as though they're waiting for supper or a poker game. Some are wearing day-glo orange vests: definitely highway workers.

A woman is busy behind the bar, the back of her head reflected in the mirrors behind the racks of liquor. She has brown, curly hair and wears a flowered T-shirt. Heads turn and eyes shift as I walk in — a nervous-looking stranger, carrying a backpack, no less. I might as well be tap-dancing.

At the bar, I introduce myself to Tina and begin stuttering out my request, but get only part of the way through before I notice the rapidly condensing bottles of beer in her hand. I invite her to deliver them, which she does. When she comes back, she tells me I probably want to see the third floor. She opens a cupboard behind the bar and plucks out a key on a green plastic doo-dad. She tells those assembled to take care of themselves for a minute while she's gone. Then she reconsiders and throws the key to a man at one of the tables. "Kenny's been around here for years, he'll show you."

A man wearing shorts and that patented southern Alberta tan stands up from his beer and jogs me across the lounge, past the pool tables, out through the industrial glass door, around the corner and up the staircase. I give him my name and tell him that I grew up a few hours north of here, not that he seems all that interested. He stops on the stairs, turns and offers his hand. "Kenny's my name. Kenny G, they call me. But I don't play the sax."

At the first landing, it's clear the old Imperial ain't what it used to be. There is water damage (isn't this part of the world going through a near biblical drought?), wrinkled carpet, worn furniture in the hallway. Light shines from under the doors to the rooms. I feel as though every crime thriller I've ever seen has been filmed right here.

"Are these rooms rented?" I ask. "Do people stay here long-term or anything?"

"Some people do," he says, continuing down the hall to a door that will lead to the third floor. We take a wrong turn — it's been a while since Kenny G's been up here — and double back toward the landing.

He slides the key in the door. I'm dying to get up there. The movie playing in my mind has shifted from prime-time crime to something featuring Clint Eastwood in chaps. I imagine well-worn wooden steps, those hanging globe lights, iron beds, leaded glass windows, hand-made lace.

Kenny wiggles the key back and forth and pushes a little on the door. No joy. "Maybe it's the wrong key." We go back to the lounge.

Tina grabs the key from him and takes over. She leads me on another trip up the stairs. People move quickly here.

She puts the key in the lock, wiggles it back and forth, pushes a little on the door. This is not going to work. "Too bad," she says. "That would have been good for you to see. It's got the old iron tubs down the hall and stuff. But it's not in its original state or anything. The previous owners put in this puke-green shag carpet. We tried to get some money to bring it back to more like what it was, but the heritage people wouldn't look at it because it was moved in from Frank."

We go back down to the lounge and Tina returns to her post. While I try to figure out what to do next, a man at Kenny G's table calls out to me. "Did she tell you about the ghost?"

This I can't resist. I wander over.

A man about my age and wearing a ball cap sits cupping a bottle of beer. He looks a little worried. "There used to be a table over there, by the door, where that pool table is. I was sitting there one afternoon, no one else with me, when I felt something whoosh behind me. I looked around, and no one was there. And the thing is, it smelled like an old man." Neither Kenny nor the other man at the table react to this. Ball Cap shows me his forearm: there are goose bumps. "Look," he says, as though pointing out an injury.

Then, from behind, Tina asks, "Do you want to see the basement? It's really old down there. I have to go anyway." I nod and she tells me to come around behind the bar. I follow her through a sliding closet door, into a storage area, and down a few decidedly creaky steps, ducking under the cross-beams to reach an earthen floor.

"They told you about the ghost, eh? I used to hate coming down here by myself. I used to sing coming down to let him know I was coming. The weird thing is, we had some old boilers down here. And when we got a new furnace a few years ago, he disappeared. No one's seen him since."

I follow her over the uneven dirt floor, past indiscernible rusty implements, a cellar door with daylight screaming through the cracks, and an entrance to a side room that looks abandoned, until we find a room with a light and boards along the wall. As Tina changes a hose on a fountain-pop canister, I tell her this place reminds me of the basement in my parents' general store, of a similar vintage, where extra cases of pop used to be stored. It makes me think the pop delivery guys in this province could get together with the historians and tell them a few things.

We go back upstairs, where Friday afternoon is tapping its finger and waving a fistful of cash at the bar. Tina is busy. I want to thank her but feel a bit foolish hanging around like this, and I don't want to impose with more questions or the dreaded notepad — rather a pathetic character trait for a writer, really. I leave.

Back in my monster truck, I head west, craving elevation, past old houses freeze-dried in the way that is only possible on the prairies. I head west past Nanton, toward the Chain Lakes, with the smell of clover through the window smooth as sweet grass. I see my first brown-eyed Susan daisies in years and happiness erupts.

What is it about this story of my great-grandparents that offers so much but gives so little? Why do I persist in this search, despite every indication there is nothing to be found? Why am I secretly relieved when I find, again and again, that nothing has stood up to the constant weathering of time? Is it because I'm spared the old cliché of the facts getting in the way of a good story? Am I happy to have my low expectations met? I don't think so. There must be something of me in all of this that I am eager to know. I can't ignore the fact that I am writing this at a time when my own identity is so uncertain: at the age of thirty-three, I have quit my job as a reporter and will begin medical school in a month.

Rainier Maria Rilke told a young poet friend, "You are so young, and I beg you to be patient toward all that is unsolved in your heart and to try to love the questions themselves ... But take whatever comes with great trust, take it upon yourself and hate nothing." This is my real roadmap.

[ix]

Hand on hand, flesh on flesh. Undershirt, apron,
suspenders, stockings. The mine singing in his
bones, and he in hers, a creaking in the trees.
A new idea takes root in the quick of her. Outside,
winter rages.

    The world does not stop, not even for a moment.

[ch. ten]

I arrive in the Pass at five in the afternoon. The numbers "100" and "2004" have been spelled out in white stones on the hill below Bellevue. Behind Hillcrest (home of "Alberta's best drinking water," a sign tells me) stands the stubble of last year's savage forest fires. The social at the Hillcrest Miners' Club is not set to begin for a couple of hours, so I have plenty of time to set myself up somewhere. The campground at Bellevue is packed with trailers and is right beside the highway, and the campground in Blairmore is full. A hotel — quite to my surprise — has rooms, but I had my heart set on pitching a tent. So I return to Hillcrest, stop in at the general store and ask the girl who works there where I might do so. She draws me a map, directs me down past the gymkana grounds, and tells me it's not a campground per se, but a nice spot by the creek where people have cleared some sites.

At the river, I find two sites — one is taken — and stand for a time in the available one trying to convince myself it's safe to sleep there. I honestly cannot say what is so unsettling about it. Maybe it's the discarded freezer pitched in the shrubs nearby. Maybe it's the possibility of bears with no one else around. Maybe it's Turtle Mountain, still ominous to me, even though the slide that decapitated it is a century old. Maybe I'm just stupid with fatigue. Either way, I find a place closer to the gymkana grounds where a walking trail opens up and pitch my tent there, in a field of bluebells. According to Aunt Kay, Rosalia was afraid of being alone. During my time as a biologist, I spent summers in places where tragedy was one cliff fall or boat accident or bear encounter away, and until now I had thought Rosalia's purported fear of being alone a little foolish. It's good for me to feel uncharacteristically clammy like this. There is a reason for these things.

I go over the questions I hope to ask old miners and their wives. What was the hierarchy among men and races and jobs in the mine? How would a Catholic in Bellevue before 1910 have heard mass? How were Slovaks regarded? What kind of foods did you eat? What did you do for fun? What rewards did you look forward to? Did the women's reform groups ever operate in the Pass? How was prostitution viewed? What was the bad winter of 1907 like?

Time to go. I drive back into town.

I'm a little late for the seven o'clock start and by the time I arrive, people have lined up down the stairs of the Miners' Club and part of the way down the block. With the exception of some of the organizers, it looks as though I'm the youngest person here by about three decades. It takes us half an hour to get to the registration desk, while long-lost friends embrace and swap friendly insults and stories of weddings and babies, diseases and deaths.

Eventually the line snakes inside, where the Miners' Club turns out to be very much like every Legion Hall I've ever been to: a glassed-in trophy case by the front entrance, a well-loved parquet dance floor, once-white ceiling tiles, a few dart boards, and a bar lined with racks of potato chips and beef jerky, behind which a bartender works feverishly, wiping the sweat from her forehead with the back of her hand.

The Coal Miners' Fun Band is on stage. A man and woman each play a fiddle, roughly in tune; there's a guitar, a bass, and a piano accordion the size of a small car. Men with finely trimmed moustaches and carefully coifed hair lead wives well used to this sort of thing onto the dance floor. Shoes slip like satin to polkas and waltzes across the buffed wood. Some of the women smile, some do not. Every one of them had a faith that moved mountains. I feel a little jealous.

The party is swinging. There's nowhere to sit, so I lean against the bar for a good while, trying to stay out of people's way and not attract too much attention, which is difficult because I am wearing the ridiculous backpack again. Soon I begin to feel as though I'm crashing someone's private party, so I pick my way back through the line-up at the front door and find my vehicle.

Earlier, I'd passed the cemetery where the victims of the 1914 Hillcrest mine explosion were buried. At the time, buzzing with plans, I hadn't felt prepared to go in. Now I am. I pull down the long treed lane and park in front of the fence, turn off my vehicle, and step out into the fading evening light. Under the ragged lip of Turtle Mountain, ringed by poplars, a wheel of stones sits waiting:

October 17, 1880 Albion Mine, Stellarton, NS
— 6 dead — drowned
February 13, 1883 Chignecto Mine, Maccan, NS
— 7 dead — suffocation
May 3, 1883 Vale Colliery, Thorburn, NS
— 7 dead — runaway trolley

Et cetera. The brotherhood of death.

I wander through the cemetery, idly noting the colours and shapes of headstones. They all face away from the mountain, as though the people who rest below have had enough of it.

The wind suddenly picks up, knocking me backwards in my shoes.

[x]

*It makes its own gravity, this idea of hers, of
theirs. Her tides run differently. Little silver fishes
swim in her veins. Sailboats, too. Trade winds
blow behind her eyes and her skin glows at night.
It takes hold and buries its toes.*

And two become three.

[ch. eleven]

Saturday morning, seven AM. The sky is bright and the sun is just coming up over the foothills to the east. There the sky is fleshy blue, like someone locked out in the cold; it deepens to the west. A sprig of dogwood grows from a split rock in the middle of the Crowsnest River, a foolish and stubborn pioneer. The water here is maybe ten metres across and shallow, cold even along the banks. In order to think, my mind needs to shout above the sound of water spilling over the scatter of ashen-grey boulders shed from Turtle Mountain. Water eddies around the massive rocks and blooms into elaborate scrolls, a permanently shifting baroque installation.

I'm right at the edge of the Turtle Mountain slide and decide to pick my way through a bit of it, before it gets too hot and the noise starts up along the not-so-distant highway. The lane leads first through trees, where every so often there is a boulder the size of a small cabin. Large poplars grow around it, oblivious as a child stretching in sleep. A crack sounds in the woods as though someone is following me. I turn to see two white-tailed deer frozen in assessment — fight or flight? — a female and a young male with velvet on his antlers. Eventually they turn and bound away, their hooves ridiculously high in the air.

Dogwoods line the road, up to my shoulders in places. There are purple asters, two and three and four blooms to a stem, copper-coloured young willow, wild roses with their jigsawed leaf edges, yarrow, tall yellow clover, goldenrod, saskatoons just setting berries now, purple vetch. The trees give way to an immense field of limestone: too quiet, too quiet. I make my way with laboured, hollow footsteps as though walking on a carpet of chalk. There are white tiger stripes in the rocks, wagon trails paved with a fine gravel of coal. Foxtails shine in the already harsh sun. Sticky, tender young birch glitter with leaves. The rocks are jagged and impossibly dry to the touch. Many have shattered under the unforgiving regime of heat and cold, a miniature of what happened hundreds of metres above. Such immensity. Not a breath of wind. A tiny wrong step in here could kill and be called revenge.

The first event I plan to attend is the 1910 Bellevue mine disaster memorial service, and that is not until eleven, so I decide to drive to Michel, where Andrew and Rosalia were married and where their baby Helen died, to see what I can see. I drive west past Crowsnest Mountain, into BC, and toward the little dot on my map that says Michel, which is surprising, considering I'd read that the place had been levelled except for the hotel. I didn't spend much time in the mountains when I was growing up in Alberta. I was a kid of the prairies, of wheat fields and vast vistas. Being here in the Rockies always makes me feel a little wiser, a little stronger, like something has been waiting for me. I drive until the creeks start running in the other direction and pass the welcome sign to Sparwood.

And there it is: the three-storey Michel Country Inn, pink as candy floss in the morning sun, cement eagles perched on the corners, a satellite dish on top, a few busted out windows, and no hint of life. But there are plants in the windows and signs that read "Open" and "World Famous Hamburgers." There are also signs that read "Closed." What's a girl to do? Cars thrum along the highway and I'm on a mission, so I stop to snap a picture and carry on.

At the tourism office in Sparwood, a clerk asks me my family name, takes down the local history book from the shelf behind the counter and flips to the Z section. "Nothing there," he says, unsurprisingly. He does tell me that both Michel and neighbouring Natal were closed by the federal government in the 1960s when it deemed the area a human health risk because of coal dust in the air. He directs me to the Michel cemetery, in what is now the Sparwood industrial park, and I head back down through the lazy valley along Michel Creek to the gate.

At the entrance there is a big sign listing the tenants. It's in no apparent order, so I scan the list, running my finger up and down the columns: Atlomare, Joseph; Grigoruk, Taras; Podrasky, Josephine; unknown, baby. So many babies. One of them Helen, long disappeared beneath the clay.

There is only one Zak, a Joseph. I find his grave, past rows of creaking pines and tilting slabs, and even one grave adorned with two saskatoon trees — one at the head, one at the feet — heavy with fruit whose temptation I feel I should avoid. "Joseph Zak, May 15, 1884 – March 1, 1956," lays under a tall tree, "Ever remembered, Ever loved." He was born two years after Andrew. But none of my Zaks had ever mentioned a Joseph. He must belong to the other family. No sign of baby Helen, who lost her life and then her name. I leave them to their peace and turn back for Alberta.

I leave my vehicle at the end of Main Street and walk down the hill to the mine, where the memorial service has already begun. I show up just as a woman from the museum is presenting the gory, tragic details — already familiar to most of those assembled — of the mine explosion in 1910. Yellow, orange, and turquoise plastic chairs are set in rows in front of the entrance to the mine, which acts as a natural amphitheatre. Many white heads and a few darker ones shade themselves against the high sun with their programs, some listening, some not. There are trays of homemade squares at the door to the museum, a water cooler, small paper tubes of sugar for those who would brave the hot coffee on a day such as today. Grasshoppers threaten to drown out those speaking at the front. Feet shuffle in the gravel. Everyone prays for a cool breeze. A retired miner sings a song in Italian. And then comes the story of the rescue.

A man in khaki shorts takes the podium and begins in a preacher's voice: "Rescue work requires a quiet kind of courage that you have to pull on with your boots each day." Some eyes in the audience look up, some look away.

"Fred Alderson was born in England. At a very early age, he decided to become a coal miner. He quickly obtained a first-class mining certificate from Newcastle-Upon-Tyne and became eligible for supervisory positions. But in 1908, Fred ventured to Canada. He was lured there by his brother who was a tipple boss out at Hosmer [BC]. He left his wife and three children in England because they were not ready to move to the wilds of Canada. Soon,

Fred was the fire boss at Hosmer." Heads nod and grasshoppers buzz as the man details Alderson's popularity, his eagerness to be part of something.

"On the evening of December 9, 1910, Hosmer mine manager Stockett received an urgent call from Bellevue. An explosion had trapped men in the mine. With no rescue stations out in Alberta, Bellevue needed help in the worst way. Stockett organized a thirteen-man team. Fred and his fellow draegermen unselfishly volunteered to help their fellow miners. The CPR volunteered a train and it raced through the valley towards Bellevue to a situation that can best be described as chaotic and disorganized. The team quickly took control of the situation.

"They carried half-hour breathing packs for any of the survivors they found. Their own supply consisted of a two-hour breathing pack. The potash packs could only supply a specific amount of purified air, and if these men overexerted themselves, they wouldn't have enough. On the first trip inside the mine, Fred had trouble with his helmet, but the problem seemed to go away. On the second trip, they made it in 9,000 feet to chute 24. There they found a group of miners barely surviving. The dragermen began to take them out one by one, out to chute 84 where the air was good, but at this time, they weren't getting enough purified air from their packs. Fred and his rescued miner collapsed in the foul air. They were found, but too late to be resuscitated."

The speaker goes on to say that Fred Alderson was buried in Hosmer, on the same day that twenty-one miners were buried in Blairmore. Hundreds of mourners gathered at his graveside, and Fred was praised in newspapers across the country.

"Ninety-four years later," the man at the mine entrance says, "one can still visit Fred's gravesite in the abandoned Hosmer cemetery. The inscription on his stone reads: 'Greater love hath no man than he lay down his life for his friends.' "

This gets me. The brotherhood of death, the brotherhood of strangers. I clear my throat and head to the museum for a glass of that water.

After the ceremony, when people have cleared away their chairs and a man in a kilt has piped us out, I run into John Kinnear. A third-generation miner living in Fernie, his father had grown up in Bellevue, and might have been my grandmother's age. I tell him my family name, but he's never heard of it. He doesn't have time to talk to me today — something in Fernie requires his immediate attention — but he says he'd love to help me in any way he can, and gives me his phone number.

We walk up the hill together, passing an older couple who are clearly labouring under the high noon sun. The woman shrugs. "I used to do this every day when I was a girl!" At the top, John and I part, and I head for the seniors' tea, where I hope to meet up with some older Slovak women from my grandmother's generation.

Inside the Bellcrest Seniors' Centre ladies and men sit at two long tables with home-baked sweets on china plates and tea in proper cups. I overhear someone say, "The people who aren't here are either dead or sick." I introduce myself to someone at the table at the front and am directed to an elderly Slovak woman selling raffle tickets for a quilt. "You speak Slovensky?" she asks. I shake my head. "Česky?" No, again.

"Pah," she says, and indicates she has little time for me. "This weekend is no good. I'm very busy here."

I say that I understand. I have crashed another party.

Outside, the town is preparing for a parade. People have staked out prime real estate with lawn chairs; girls in scratchy dresses are looking around to see if they're being watched. "You might want to move your car," someone tells me. "You're going to be pelted with candy." I wander off to find my vehicle, tucked neatly in front of a new "No Parking" sign.

[xi]

*It begins like anything, with a sense that perhaps
you should have noticed it sooner, when you were
folding laundry or milking the cow. In days, her
throat becomes a battleground. Tiny daggers
stud the space that is not quite nose and not quite
tongue. She dries like a desert. The little fishes
gasp for air. Even her heart begins to complain,
wrestling with itself in the cage of her chest.*

[ch. twelve]

At some point during the day someone recommended that I speak to Orestes Serra, one of the oldest people in the area. He grew up in Bellevue and is said to be sharp as a tack. He's living over in the nursing home in Blairmore, which is convenient, because I know that a certain Joseph Zak, son of Henry Zak Jr. who owned the store in Coleman, is living there, too. I decide there is little use relying on opportunistic interviews anymore. People are too busy re-living their memories here this weekend to want to talk about them with some stranger who claims to be related to a family no one seems to have heard of. I drive to the nursing home.

On the business side of alarm-coded doors, a nurse tells me that Mr. Serra is sleeping, and instead shows me to the room of "Jo Jo" Zak. A man in a wheelchair and red cap is sitting beside his bed watching a golf game on TV. I thank the nurse and introduce myself.

"Andrew Zak?" he asks. "Never heard of him. My father was Henry. Never mentioned an Andrew. And what was her name?"

No use. Not even someone with the same last name has any recollection of my family. Not even a man with a family resemblance so strong he could pass for my Uncle Johnny with twenty years on him. I mentioned the Joseph Zak in the Michel cemetery; Jo Jo hadn't heard of him, either. I suppose it makes sense. These towns were relatively isolated. Tourism is a new invention here. We chat about his life and mine, about how he lost his leg in the war and took a bullet that sculpted his left hand. I make to leave and he tells me to stay a bit longer, that old Orestes won't be awake yet, but soon. We visit a little longer, then I say goodbye.

Orestes Serra is still sleeping, but a nurse says, "He won't mind being woken up, not for a visit." I tell the nurse he's never met me. "Doesn't matter," she says. "He loves visitors."

It's true. Orestes loves visitors. I give him a few minutes to collect himself after the nurse wakes him up, then I enter his room to find him in a white T-shirt, plaid shirt, cardigan, and polar fleece pants pulled up higher than I thought possible. His eyes are very blue and his skin is very smooth; an electric shaver sits plugged in at his bedside. I tell him it's very gracious of him to talk to me, especially with no notice I was coming.

"It is my gift to my creator," he says grandly. "When people want to know about history, it's my duty to help them. I am not just me, an individual. I am part of a community. I have to help."

My lucky day. He tells me he was born in 1904, which makes him three years older than my grandmother would have been.

My tape recorder malfunctions and I lose most of the details of our conversation. But he gives me some answers to specific questions I'd had: yes, it was common for people to live in Bellevue but work in Hillcrest; even before a school was built in Bellevue, classes were held in converted houses owned by the WCC; before a church was built, the Catholic priest from Coleman would say mass in Bellevue; the sidewalks were boards; if people wanted to travel between towns, it was normal to walk in at least one direction because trains were infrequent and cost money; racially motivated fights were more common on paydays when the men got drunk. He tells me his own father, a shoemaker from Italy, came to the region and eventually became a blacksmith. They kept three cows, and other families with too many babies to take care of their own milk needs would "order a cow" from them: the Serras would bring the cow to and from pasture every day, and all the milk that cow produced would go to that family.

Orestes has an easy nature. As we've been talking, his chair has crept a little closer and a little closer until his leg is resting against mine. His smiles are many. He is mere months from his one hundredth birthday.

"You're an optimistic person," I tell him.

"My long life is a big thank-you to my creator. It's a good life."

It's evening now, and I'm starting to despair a little that my research has turned up so little in the way of family details or historical reconstruction. But I reassure myself that the other reason for my trip is to simply breathe the air, to imagine bodily what the world was like here one hundred years ago. Both Grandma and Mrs. Fontana told me about walking in hills to collect cows out on common pasture. So that's where I go next.

At first, I have a hard time finding somewhere to walk that's not fenced off with big "No Trespassing" signs. But finally, at the west end of town, I see a trail and check with a man standing in his yard nearby. He tells me I can walk all the way to Frank along that road if I am so inclined. I park my beast and get out into the mountain air.

Finally, peace. Quiet, crisp air. A partly overgrown wagon trail. Lodgepole pines with cones like tiny fists. Meadows above the ragged treeline. A cow's laboured mooing carrying through the valley. Strange flowers, like little heads of purple dreadlocks, everywhere. Twigs breaking under the weight of something heavy. Blonde dirt, fine as smoke. The sun like a shirt on my back, and the stones warm and dry. Thunder rolling over from the northeast. And no matter where I go, Turtle Mountain staring down at me like a sinister man.

[xii]

She awakens one day to find she can breathe
again. She is as weak as a cooked noodle.

Ideas do not flourish in noodles. She loses
the baby.

Still, because one day must follow the next,
she drinks and rests and drinks and rests, and
then one day it's the laundry, and another it's the
milking, and weeks pass and still no blood. Life
begins again. One day later still, something rolls
over inside her and gives itself a little stretch.

[ch. thirteen]

In spite of suggestions from my family that it may be fruitless, it seems time to pay a visit to Annie, Grandma's sister and Rosalia's only living child, whom I have never met. Mom recommends I take Aunt Julie, who has maintained some contact with her. I call Aunt Julie and we agree I will go to Red Deer the next morning, pick her up at ten, and go to The Pines seniors' home, where Annie lives. Should we call ahead, I wonder? Aunt Julie figures it'll be okay just to show up. As long as she's still there, of course, it's been a while.

The next morning, I am uncharacteristically punctual and show up at ten on the dot. We have a bit of tea and play with Aunt Julie's budgie before setting out. In the parking lot of the seniors' home, I tell Aunt Julie that I am most interested in learning about Andrew and Rosalia's earliest years. "I know Grandma was born and raised in Bellevue, but I don't know when they moved there," I say. "I don't know where they lived before, or why they would have moved."

"Well, Mother wasn't born in Bellevue," Aunt Julie corrects me. "She was born in Hosmer."

Well, then. Aunt Julie tells me she knows nothing more than that, though, and we enter the home.

We see Anna Trennaman's name on the list of occupants in the front lobby and walk down the nearest hallway. But at room 302, it's not her at all. We stick our heads into the beauty salon and ask directions, thinking we're in the wrong wing. "Anna?" says the hairdresser. "She's not here anymore. She left a couple of months ago to be closer to her daughter down south somewhere."

A stop at the administrator's office confirms Annie has moved to Coaldale, where she's living in Sunny South Lodge. "She's ninety-four," the woman in head office tells us in response to our queries about her health. "She has her good days and bad days. Like all of us, I suppose."

Back at home in Elnora, I tell Mom about my trip to Red Deer. "I have some papers in my safe deposit box," she tells me. "I'll go to the bank this afternoon. Remind me."

No need, though. She goes straight uptown and returns in a few minutes with a tattered envelope containing two yellowed documents: the baptismal certificate of her father, John Pisko, and the marriage certificate of her parents, dated October 16, 1923:

	BRIDEGROOM	BRIDE
Name in Full	John Pisko	Emma Helen Zak
Place of Residence	Mountain Park, Alberta	Delburne, Alberta
Place of Birth	Helsmanovci, Czechoslovakia	Hosmer, BC
Age	Twenty Five Years	Sixteen Years
Names of Parents	Father Peter Pisko Mother Martha Burchak	Father Andrew Zak Mother Rosie Patala

John must have met the family when they lived in Mountain Park, before they moved to the homestead in Delburne in 1919. Grandma would have been twelve.

Andrew and Rosalia moved around much more than I had imagined, having married and had their first child in Michel, then moving on to Hosmer a year later, and onto Bellevue where Uncle Tom was born, by 1914.

Piece by tiny piece, the picture comes together.

[xiii]

The bread will not rise. She kneads and pounds
and coaxes the creature with extra yeast. She
kisses it. She performs animal sacrifices She takes
it to bed and tucks it in near her feet, like a dog.
She calls on the ghost of her dead grandmother.

   Still, the bread will not rise.

   When everything has failed and she would walk
into the river if not for her passenger, she finds a
neighbour to invite for tea.

   Their laughter catches in the gassy caverns
of dough and the bread swells and swells.

[ch. fourteen]

That box of stuff at Ken's place is starting to eat at me. I'm dying to know what's in there. On a bright Friday morning, I phone and catch him at work in his back yard, tell him I'll be up within the hour, and borrow Mom's car.

The old Zak place is four miles east and south of Delburne. The only two Zaks who stayed on the land in this area were my grandmother, Helen, and her little brother Tom. Both are gone now, but their children have stayed and multiplied and built modest but sufficient farms. Even kids who'd been away from it for years — sisters Brenda, a chartered accountant in Edmonton, and Jan, who has come home and married a local guy after years in Nova Scotia — have returned to the farming saddle.

Ken Zak (son of Tom), along with his wife Linda, now live on Andrew and Rosalia's original homestead. I turn off down the gravel range road, putt along behind a tractor for a bit, then enter their long, treed lane leading to the top of gentle hill.

Linda, a famously friendly elementary school teacher in Delburne, greets me in the driveway and pulls off their dog. Ken joins us, fiddling with an unlit, half-smoked cigarette. We talk about puppies and where last night's tornadoes touched down, then go in the house.

Five small ivory envelopes sit in a neat pile at the head of the kitchen table. "That's what was in the box. There wasn't much."

"Not to worry," I say, thinking to myself, "It's the story of this story."

Ken heads straight for the unmarked envelope. Inside are five three-by-four-and-a-half-inch prints and four negatives of someone's funeral. In one photo, six men stand with hats in hand at the open end of a hearse. There is a shiny black car parked behind; a woman sits on the passenger seat with her jacketed arm out the window. Three young boys in ill-fitting suits and short, short haircuts stand with heads bowed, their long shadows just touching the edge of a freshly dug grave. Another shows six men positioned along the sides of a rather grand coffin, stepping off the wooden steps of a country church into shin-deep grass; two little girls — one with shiny ringlets and another, smaller one with two fastidious French braids, both in white dresses — hold hands as they watch the procession. There's another photo of the coffin being lowered into its resting spot, and so on.

"Uncle Tony's funeral," Ken says. "He died in a mining accident in Cadomin on April 25, 1934. Most of these papers have to do with his insurance claim."

He opens another envelope and hands me a stiff piece of paper. "Not a very flattering likeness, I suppose."

Uncle Tony lies surrounded by a cloud of white satin under the open lid of his coffin. He has a prominent brow, bushy eyebrows, a wide nose, and a wide mouth with a heavy bottom lip. Hard to get a good sense of what the live man looks like from the dead, I suppose. I turn the photo over. It's a postcard. "Made in Canada" it says, with spaces marked "Correspondence" and "Place Stamp Here."

"I asked Father Paul why they did that," Ken says, noticing my bewilderment. "He said it was to prove someone was really dead. Sometimes they used to have to exhume graves to prove to Aunt So-and-so that someone was really gone. I guess this saved a lot of trouble."

He hands me a second postcard of three mourners standing beside a coffin, likely Tony's, although it's hard to know for sure.

"Don't know who they are," Ken says.

Not Rosalia and Andrew, though?

"Nope."

The postcards came from an envelope containing a letter handwritten in Slovak on small pieces of blue-lined paper. A second letter is also written in Slovak, this one in a hand less sure, and on ivory paper translucent as onion skin. The final envelope contains a letter from the Mutual Life Assurance Company of Canada office in Edmonton, dated August 22, 1934:

Mrs. Rozalia Zak,
Delburne, Alta.

Dear Madame:
Re: Policy No. 59 — Certificate No. 358
T. Trstensky Deceased.

We wish to attach hereto the companies (sic) cheque
for $1,006.52, representing the face amount of the above
numbered Certificate, together with the accrued interest
on the proceeds.

Yours very truly,
(signed G.A. Guthrie)
Branch Secretary.

I make some kind of remark like, "So that's what a life comes to," but Linda stops me.

"That was an awful lot of money back then. It was the Depression." It's true, I suppose. Later, out of curiosity, I look up on a Statistics Canada inflation converter today's equivalent of a thousand dollars during the Depression: $14,453.49. Still doesn't seem like much.

The letters and things, though not much in the way of volume or content, turn out to be excellent prompts for Ken and Linda.

"Grandad was a small guy," Ken begins. "Most miners were. He was four-foot-something, and not much more than a hundred pounds. About your size, I guess. He went to school in a monastery. You see, his dad died when he was three, and his mother and sister died when he was twelve."

"Some kind of flu epidemic," Linda adds.

"He remembered his grandmother being a good cook." I remind Ken about the plums and he chuckles. "He left school when he was fourteen. At that time, he had to decide whether he wanted to commit to the monastery for good, and I guess he decided that wasn't for him. He started selling glass from town to town."

I tell Ken and Linda about my being amazed to learn it was plate glass he was selling, not just trinkets that mere mortals might have been able to carry.

"No, no. Plate glass." Linda nods in mutual amazement. "He used to carry his glass and his putty and his wedges all around. I suppose he would have had them on a board and lashed them to that. Then he put it on his back and walked. He said he took up smoking then. It would make him dizzy so he could forget about the hunger and go to sleep. Tobacco was only a penny a pound, and food, well ..."

Ken jumps in. "He had a dealer who would meet him along the road with new supplies. He walked into Russia and Belarus. I heard he learned six different languages."

A fourteen-year-old boy burying his wallet at the edge of town so he wouldn't be robbed, and walking into imperial Russia to repair broken windows. When I was fourteen, my major concerns were what to do with my hair, new pimples, and failing to learn my lines in *Rebel Without a Cause* for our Grade Ten drama production. Andrew would have been a man before his voice had broken.

"He came here with a brother. Christopher, I think he said his name was. But he didn't stay long. He went back to the old country and died of appendicitis."

I have so many questions it's hard to keep them in any workable order. "Do you think he intended to start mining when he came here?"

"I don't think so," Ken answers.

"Remember him making up that story?" Linda smiles.

"Oh yeah. He had never mined before in the old country. But he went to some mine office, and when they asked if he had any experience, he just remembered the name of a mining company he'd heard of back home and said he'd worked for them! That was enough, I guess."

Then I ask, "Why do you think that someone who dropped his old life in a farming and mining community to sail around the world to a new country seeking opportunity would have found himself farming and mining?"

"Well, you've got to think that he had no one at home." Ken begins. "His parents were gone. There was hunger. Even Mom talked about hunger. There was the lure of Canada, free land."

Linda jumps in. "And there were a lot of Slovaks in the mines. If you don't speak the local language, you're going to fall in with people you can talk to. It'd be just like if I went somewhere and some Canadian took me aside."

"He was eighteen when he came," Ken adds, confirming Aunt Cec's recollection that he had come around 1901.

I ask about Tony then. Did he and Andrew know each other in Slovakia? What role did Tony play in hooking Andrew up with Rosalia?

"They didn't know each other over there, they met in the Pass. I think they moved around from mine to mine with each other. Tony told Granddad about his niece living down in New York, and they started corresponding." Ken smiles, the romance of the story apparently not lost on him either. "I suppose he said to her, 'Why don't you come up here and check me out?' I think he sent her the fare. Tony would have vouched for him."

I tell them Rosalia's immigration papers indicate she arrived in New York in 1902. She married Andrew in Michel, BC, in 1905. How long was she in New York? How long did she and Andrew correspond? How long was she in the Pass before she and Andrew married?

Neither Ken nor Linda knows. Is it out of modesty and privacy that Andrew and Rosalia never spoke about their early courting years? Or did later hardships make them forget there was ever a time that they had chosen each other?

Ken returns me to terra firma. "Tony and Granddad were really close. He taught Granddad how to hunt and fish, because Granddad just spent all his time in the mine. And Uncle Tony helped out here a lot. Granddad came up in 1919, and Tony and some of his friends helped him clear that field there." Ken motions over his shoulder to an invisible quarter-section. "They just came and pitched a tent. They cleared it with axes. I suppose they had nothing better to do. And back then, it wasn't so much about 'this is mine and this is yours.' People helped one another. It was a survival mentality, I think. And maybe it had to do with everybody being a little related, who knows?"

Ken was four when Andrew died in 1959. A little young to remember much about someone's personality, likes and dislikes, but I ask anyway.

"I remember he didn't like little kids very much," he chuckles. "He sure didn't like me patting him on the head."

"But he was sick," Linda reminds us, ever ready with humanity. "He had arthritis and cancer. He had lumps all over. He was probably sore all day. But he still worked hard. He'd be out there in the back yard cutting the grass with a scythe. He'd plant potatoes as soon as the snow was gone, at the end of April, not even May. I guess he thought 'If we have nothing else, we'll have potatoes.'"

Did he ever give up smoking?

"He was down to four a day when he died," Ken smiles, still fingering his half cigarette. He pauses for a minute.

"They used to get dressed up to the nines to go to church. He was very devout. If he wasn't shaved by sunset on Saturday, he went to church unshaven."

"Because you're supposed to do no work on Sunday?" I ask, the religious novice.

"No, because of vanity," Ken corrects me. "You're supposed to practice no vanity on the Sabbath. Just like you're supposed to wear no perfume. All the men wore pin-striped suits and fedoras."

"Andrew wore a fedora?" Linda smiles.

"Granddad wore a fedora." Ken affirms. "To church."

He and Tony continued mining after Andrew came to Delburne. Like many men in the area, when the fields were cleared for winter, and when demand for coal was at its peak, farmers went back underground. Andrew worked in Drumheller and at a mine in Ardley, north of Delburne. He was a contract miner, which meant he bought his own powder and fuses and was paid by the ton. From Delburne, he'd hop the train south to Drumheller, where he'd work for three days, then ride the train back north to Ardley for three days, and be home for Sunday. During the Depression he was making $73 every week; my Stats Can calculator tells me that's nearly $900 by today's standards. Not too shabby. In 1929, he bought another quarter-section, and co-signed on another one for his daughter Helen, married already six years to John Pisko. Andrew Zak wasn't a poor man, but he worked — the labour of another generation almost requires an altogether different word — for everything his family had.

Ken, Linda, and I have a cup of tea, and then I leave. Back on the main gravel road, I stop to survey the vast country now owned by Andrew and Rosalia's descendants.

All begun with a photograph and a wild hope.

[xiv]

It came in the night, bending her double. Even

he, whose days were littered with dismemberment

and death, and was accustomed to the parting

of flesh, could not bear the animal howls. He went

outside, as anyone might, to chop wood. And when

the thing was done, there lay the future, purple as

a clenched fist.

[ch. fifteen]

I'm driving to the Pass again, for the second time in as many weeks. I'm starting to anticipate certain landmarks along the highway, along with the opportunity to stop in at what's become my favourite coffee shop.

My attempts to reach Aunt Annie earlier in the week had failed. I called the seniors' home in Coaldale and had a conversation that ran something like this:

"Hello."

"Hello! I'm looking for Anna Trennamen."

"I'm sorry, I can't give any information about residents."

"Oh, but my aunt and I stopped in to visit her in Red Deer, and they said she'd moved in with you, to be closer to her daughter Joyce."

"I'm sorry, I can't give any information about residents. You'll have to go through family or try directory assistance."

"I am family. And I tried directory assistance. There's no listing."

"I'm sorry, you'll have to go through family."

"I am fa — Okay. Can you at least give her a message and ask her to call me?"

"I'm sorry. I can't give any informa — "

"Thanks." Click. *For nothing,* I think savagely.

I called directory assistance then, looking for Annie's daughter. The only matching name I could find had no idea who I was, and she was not, she told me, the daughter of Anna Trennamen. Okay. I can take a hint. Eventually.

So I have taken a pass on Coledale, and am now heading for Coleman. (Even a Martian would surmise the history of this place, going on its place name alone.) Again, I am to meet Caron Townsend, this time at the coffee shop. I'm not certain I'll recognize her, but as I slow to signal and pull the car into the parking lot, I find myself directly behind an old blue Olds. We each park our cars and she gets out smiling, carrying a *Coleman Centennial Cookbook, 1904 – 2004: Ethnic and Family Favourites.* It's for me. Inside, we get reacquainted and arrange to go to our first interview.

We park our cars by a back alley, pass through a wire gate into a lush back garden, and walk up a flight of wooden stairs to a back door, where Caron knocks perfunctorily and lets us in to a kitchen. Irene Wood, a woman of ninety-four years and the sole occupant and caretaker of the house, calls from the back room, strides across the carpeted floor, and steps down onto the linoleum. She's a tiny woman with white hair. She wears a white cardigan and is standing in a very white, freshly scrubbed kitchen. Before we can say hello she is already telling us not to expect much from her. Someone was here this summer to ask about the war, and she is just no good with dates. She leads us into the living room. Even darkened as it is against the afternoon sun, her home is obviously immaculate.

"The dates I'm not very clear on," she begins apologizing again, even before I can tell her what I am interested in knowing. "In those days you didn't pay much attention to dates. Except if you had a date with a fella. And that was a long time coming!"

Both of Irene's parents came from northern Italy, although from different towns. They met and married in the Pass in 1908, three years after Rosalia and Andrew married in Michel. In the early years, Irene's father worked as foreman for the CPR, then for a liquor store in Blairmore. When that went out of business, he bought the building. In 1914, when Irene was four years old, he opened the Chinook Ice Cream Parlour.

"You must have been the most popular kid in town."

"I remember that ice cream parlour was quite busy," she chuckles. "In those days, they had the Sanatorium where the soldiers came to recuperate. They used to spend a lot of time up at the store. We had a player piano in there, and we used to put a nickel in it to make it play." One night, when the power bumped, the piano played through the night; still, she can't remember the tunes. Irene's father's business ventures soon expanded. He closed the ice cream parlour and became an agent for beer and pop sales, eventually opening his own bottling plant. He had no sons to help him and clearly had a plan for young Irene.

"When I was in Grade Ten, I got shipped to Calgary to the convent to finish my high school and take a business course. When I graduated, the teacher and the principal told me that they had a job in Calgary for me. But I didn't like Calgary. I was so homesick. I came home for the holidays and I told my mother and dad that I wanted to stay. By this time, my dad had opened the Red & White chain store, and he thought I could run the business for him. So I did. I ran the Red & White chain store for five years."

I quickly did the math: that meant Irene ran a business as a young single woman during the years of the Depression. Tough lady.

"The only thing I wouldn't do for my dad is his bookkeeping. He had his own system. I did everything else. I did the buying and everything for the store. The stores were always closed on Wednesday afternoons. And Sundays, of course, in those days. Monday to Friday, we worked until between five and six. And on Saturday nights, it was nine o'clock. And a lot of Italians came into our store because they could speak Italian that way. If they went to Thompsons, they'd have to speak English."

A remarkable experience at a time when Irene says the only women who worked outside the home were teachers and nurses.

It lasted five years, until she got married. After that, Irene would go down to the store only on weekends, or during a big sale. Sometimes she would help out in the bottling plant, too, setting up the bottles to wash and fill. Her father hoped she and her husband would buy the plant one day and thought it would be good practice for her to know the operation intimately. But they never did buy it.

Irene was a contemporary of my grandmother, but clearly she had a very different experience of the Pass as a member of the merchant class. Then I remember the strikes: mine workers had no money then, and I know very well from my own parents' experience of running a grocery store in a village that when local people have no money, as in a bad crop year, food is often one of the first places they'll cut corners.

"The strikes were pretty tough," she agrees. "But there was one thing about my dad that I will say — and I'm very proud of this fact — if a person came in that had a family and they were hungry, my dad would always give them credit. When he was building the plant, my dad asked some of the men if they would like to come and help with the building and he would take it off their bills. And there was lots that did. I can remember lots of times I would say to my dad, 'This one would like some credit,' and he would say, 'Give it to her, maybe the children are hungry.' I can always remember that part."

A few days earlier, when my mother and I had taken a trip into Red Deer, Mom noticed a woman who used to live in Elnora walking down the sidewalk. The woman still owed the family store about one hundred dollars. A hundred bucks is a good portion of a day's deposit at the store, and I asked Mom if she thought she'd ever see the money again. "Well, her kids came in just before Easter one time and said their mom had spent her cheque on booze, and they had nothing to cook for Easter dinner. I don't know if it's true or not." She'd shrugged. "I figure I bought the kids Easter dinner." I felt very proud of my mom just then. I could relate to what Irene was saying about her father.

I was curious about whether there were any official aid groups in the Pass, any early food banks such as the one in Blairmore now.

"Not that I know of in those days. I can't ever remember anyone being fed or anything. But there was lots of people who would help people. Because I know there was a poor family who lived close to our house and my mother would give them anything we grew out of. A lot of people helped that way. And in those days, like when we lived across the track, there was a lot of poor people. And of course with my dad being in business, I had a sleigh that I could go down the hill. But all my friends couldn't afford it. They used to go down in cardboard boxes. I wouldn't bring my sleigh over there because I thought maybe they'd think I was showing off. So I used to go in cardboard boxes with them. I would do what they did because I didn't want them to think that I was better than they were or something. It was very hard in those days when the mine wasn't working. And there was not any other industry here at the time. You used to have to wait until four o'clock to see whether there was going to be no whistles or three whistles. If there were three whistles, that meant there was no work the next day."

With hungry babies at home, four o'clock must have come as daily judgement.

A couple of blocks away, over at Julie Lant's house, Caron and I find a small woman in a kitchen nook watching the afternoon soaps on a television suspended from a cupboard, patiently delaying her trip downtown to wait for us to show up. We're late and she seems a bit put off at first, excusing herself to retrieve her hearing aids. But Julie, I soon learn, is not a woman to rest on pleasantries.

"My dad came to this country in 1903," she says, settling down at the table again and beginning in on the family bio. "He came from Italy. He worked for the CPR, laying track for a dollar a day. My mom was sixteen when she came over to Canada from Italy. She was seventeen when she met my dad and they were married. He had three children from a previous marriage—his wife had passed away—so my mom was seventeen and raised these three small children, and then she had ten children of her own."

Julie was the second, born in 1925; her brothers and sisters came every year and a half after that. The midwife—"old lady Amatto" from across the street—would come and spend all day if she needed to. The kids were shipped off to their grandmother's for the day, to leave Mrs. Amatto to the boiling of water and sheets (always white, because any other colour couldn't be bleached). She was never paid with cash—there was none. Julie's father had a big garden, and instead would load up the midwife with produce.

"Mom baked twenty-eight loaves of bread every day—she had growing boys. It was an all-day job, really. You could put about six loaves at a time in the old coal ovens, eh? And there was no washing machines. You scrubbed everything by hand and you hung everything in the house in the winter because it froze outside. There were lines everywhere, over the old wood stove. No one ever got colds in those days because of the moisture in the house. And you had outside facilities. We used to have a tunnel from the house to the toilet. The light would come through the snow, the white snow. And it was warm. We loved it in there. If you wanted to go out and play when it was twenty and thirty below, you got rubbed with goose grease as protection, under your clothes."

This is more like the story I had imagined for my own family.

"We had chickens. We had a garden. And my dad used to go hunting. For deer, elk, moose, porcupine. Porcupine is good meat. It's light. It made good spaghetti sauce. And he never had sleeping bags in those days. He had old overcoats and he covered himself with those. No tents, either. They slept under the trees."

Despite their modest resources, Christmas was a big deal for Mrs. Lant's family. Her mother would make each of the girls a new doll on her treadle sewing machine, and the boys a new shirt. Each would get an orange. And there was music: the boys played guitar, her mom played accordion, the girls all sang, and everyone danced. The day after Christmas, Julie's father would line up all the children and feed everyone a tablespoon of castor oil. "To clean us out," Julie explains. "And if you were the last in the line, you were in agony. You were gagging."

I ask Julie if her mother ever got involved with any ladies' organizations.

"She never had time. The women who were in those, they were well-to-do. Lawyers' wives. Someone else at home doing the work. No, if someone was sick, Mom would make three or four loaves of bread for them and a pot of soup. That's the way they helped each other."

Were the women's reform groups, the Women's Christian Temperance Union and the Alberta Moral Reform League, ever active in the Pass?

"No, because everyone relied on Picariello." Emilio "The Emperor" Picariello was one of southern Alberta's best-known rum runners during the Prohibition years. In 1923, he was hanged for a murder many in the Pass—including Julie—believe he didn't commit.

"My dad was one of the rum runners. He used to drive cars to the border down by Cardston. Mom used to get things from Picariello. He'd pack the booze in flour and sugar, then give that to the bigger families. He was like a Robin Hood. He fed every family. My dad ran the beer parlour for him after, and they became really friendly. So then he was my brother Rossie's godfather. Every Saturday he used to take Rossie and all his little friends to the show, paid their way to the show. My brother never forgot that. Picariello looked after everybody. He didn't deserve to die."

Nor would it seem that many in the Pass supported the reformers' vehement opposition to prostitution. According to Julie and Caron, a particular facility on nearby Goat Mountain was viewed as a necessary part of civilized society.

Caron: "My mom was a nurse. She was working when the house was open. The ladies used to come in to the doctor's every month to get checked."

Julie: "There were five of them. They came on Wednesdays. When I was expecting the twins, I used to go for my check-up on a Wednesday, and the doctor would tell me, 'You come in the afternoon, because in the morning, that's when the ladies are here.'"

Caron: "If they had a problem —"

I interrupt and ask Caron if by "problem" she meant a sexually transmitted disease or a pregnancy.

"Well, an STD. No, a pregnancy, they got rid of that. There were ways and means of doing it. But if they had a problem, then they were taken off the circuit and they were cured and they could go back to work. But when you think about it, a lot of people said rape wasn't as prevalent because the men had somewhere to go. And you had a lot of single miners. Because they would come and leave the families over there, and they would try to save enough money to bring them. So it had its place."

Julie: "Yeah, it's too bad that they closed down places like that. There's so many teenage pregnancies."

Caron: "And now you've got them wandering the streets. The girls you see on the streets, it's sad."

I wonder aloud who the women of Goat Mountain were. "They were actually nice ladies," Julie says. "They never bothered anybody. It was run like a business. Certain ones would go and do the shopping. They had a man to do maintenance on the house. They had their own little bridge across the river. My husband used to drive a taxi." She chuckles, for the first time during our conversation. "He used to drive a lot of prominent businessmen there."

Every time I've talked with people about the past, I have been regaled with stories of hard work and good times in the face of misery. These I have come to expect. But I have never had two women — nearly strangers, and of another generation — speak candidly to me in support of rum running and prostitution. It makes me smile. Gutsy ladies, then and now.

I ask Julie if her parents seemed happy, or if they ever talked about going back to Italy.

"No. They loved it here," she says without elaborating.

"Did they ever talk about why?" I ask. "Just more freedom, or —"

"Well, they didn't have the money to go, for one thing. They always talked about the old country. But they never planned on going. It's not like nowadays when people pick up and go. They couldn't do it."

"Did they ever get back to visit?"

"No."

"Have you ever been?"

"No."

"And your mom, do you know if she was fairly content, or was she tired, or —"

"She'd go to bed and she was tired. But she never complained. She always made good meals. It was always roast or stew or spaghetti. And when it was our birthdays, Mom had this great big pan, and she always made a walnut cake. A great big walnut cake, and there was no fancy icing or anything. But we had a fancy cake. She was happy raising her family."

Just like any other woman.

[xv]

A star blinks out when a baby dies.

They buried her in the cold ground and tried
to remember to breathe.

What else can be said about such matters?

[ch. sixteen]

After saying goodbye to Caron in Coleman, I head toward BC. This time I'm bound for Hosmer, where I think Rosalia and Andrew lived in 1907, since this is where my grandmother was born. John Kinnear has told me to meet him at the Hosmer Hotel, where we'll talk for a bit, then go for a walk around some of the mine ruins.

I arrive in Hosmer and find a tavern with one truck parked in the dust out front. There's a small veranda, and through the porch, a sign on the inner, windowless door reads: "Come in, this is a smoking place."

Inside, as usual carrying my backpack, I feel immediately conspicuous. Two people sit at a long wooden table watching *Jeopardy!* on television. A scruffy dog hunkers by their feet. The older man gets up from the table. "Can I help you?" he asks.

"This the Hosmer Hotel?"

"The one and only."

I take a table at what I hope is a respectful, rather than aloof, distance from the occupied one. I sit down on a vinyl chair, drop my bag in the next one, and look around. As the bartender gets my drink, he tells me there's some pretty decent chili in the corner and that I can help myself.

The place is wallpapered with beer coasters from various companies and countries. A genuine ball and chain hangs near the door. Above the entrance to the washrooms is a wooden sign engraved with the instructions "4U2P." There is a pool table and a shuffleboard table. A coffee pot engaged in an asthmatic monologue sits on the end of the counter. A pegboard sign near the television reads:

> Beer $2.50
> Bizarre Beer $3.50

I like it here.

I watch TV for a bit, until the door opens and John Kinnear walks in. He's just off work, riding around on an all-terrain vehicle reading global positioning system co-ordinates for the area coal company; it's good of him to meet me here in my narrow window of opportunity. Seeing that I've ordered a drink, he decides to join me for one.

John has already been kind enough to point me in the way of some BC history, but what I really want to know from him is whether he can divine from the few dates I have of my family's history why Andrew and Rosalia might have moved when they did, and whether there are any hints about their earliest years — where Andrew worked when he first came to the Pass. I go over the salient facts again.

"I know Andrew came to Canada in 1900, and have no evidence he went anywhere else other than the Pass. I know Rosalia emigrated to New York in 1902, and that she married Andrew in Michel in 1905. I know they stayed there for at least a year, because their first child died there in 1906. They moved to Hosmer by 1907, because that's where their next child, my grandmother, was born. They were in Bellevue by 1914 at the latest, because that's where Grandma's little brother was born. Does any of that make sense to you?"

John barely hesitates. "Well, the railway was pushed through in 1898, and very soon after that, Fernie had coal from the Coal Creek mine ready to ship. So he might have worked there. But Natal and Michel were already developing by 1901. The first tipples were built in 1902. So I'd say he was either working in Fernie or Michel. But it's hard to say. Depends on what kind of work he was into. The Slovaks were good miners, given their stocky build — "

"Turns out he was my size," I interrupt.

"Your size?"

"Yeah. A short little bugger. Maybe even smaller than me." I had told John earlier that Andrew was Slovak, and he'd told me about Slovak miners he'd worked with who had forearms the size of a smallish thigh. He's having trouble picturing my great-grandfather as a small man.

"Oh. Well, maybe he was a labourer. In that case, he was likely in Michel, working on getting the new mine ready."

"But I know he was eventually a miner. A good one, too, I'm told."

"Really?"

"Made good money later on in Drumheller." I continue, "Okay, either Fernie or Michel before he married. Then a move to Hosmer in 1907. Any idea why?"

"Well, Hosmer was being built in 1906. That was a CPR operation, and the CPR was the last in the game. You see, as part of the Crowsnest Pass Agreement in 1898, the CPR agreed it would not mine its own coal for ten years, and instead buy its coal from area companies. It only operated the mine in Hosmer until 1914. It shut it down for economic reasons. But I don't know why someone would want to move from an established mine in Michel to Hosmer. The rates were about the same. Again, I suppose it's a question of the kind of work he did. There was a lot of concrete being poured in 1906 – 1907, a lot of stonework construction."

John is genuinely perplexed. Then something occurs to him. "What kind of guy was he? Did he get along with people? You think he might have been fired?"

I smile. A Zak lose his temper? Never.

From the hotel, we pile into John's truck and rattle off in failing afternoon light through the dense mixed wood forest and down an old track toward a construction project of which he's very proud. Soon, the trail widens and we park to have a closer look. In the side of a grassy embankment ten or so feet high is a long row of stone facings of various dimension and states of preserve: beehive coke ovens shaped like igloos, with a flat stone floor and a hole in the top. A coal car used to run along the top, charging the ovens with seven tons of slack coal where it would burn for several hours under low-oxygen conditions. Then it would be quenched with water, raked out, and loaded by pitchfork into waiting box or ore cars. "Pulling ovens" was hot work, at $1.50 per oven. They made good business sense for CNP Coal: coke was in demand at steel mills across

America, and the company made use of coal chunks that were too small to sell.

A few years back, John and some friends grew concerned — and protective — about the crumbling mine infrastructure in Hosmer that got a federal government grant to help preserve it. Local people were hired to clear shrub and excavate and cut new stone to shore up the crumbing walls. John says it was difficult to keep the structures absolutely historically accurate, but the work has, at the very least, helped protect the bank of ovens, the condition of which now shows a full spectrum from nearly decayed to fully restored. He leads me down the lane, pointing out little drifts of coal here, animal tracks there. We come to a break in the bank where a lane has been cut. On top of the excavated face sits a massive tree whose roots have worked their deliberate way through the century-old bricks, crooked as fingers curled in sand.

"We left that," he smiles. "I've taken lots of pictures of that tree. There's just something about it."

Around the back, we work our way through denser vegetation, stopping to pick at wild raspberries and saskatoons and to admire the dark entrances. I'm a bit claustrophobic, but instead of feeling sucked off balance, as I often do in front of deep, dark spaces, these ovens suggest to me shelter. They seem immovable, kiva-like. Perhaps it is John's obvious reverence for them.

We jump back in the truck and John whisks us further up the mountainside on another track. "Good," he says, spying an open gate. We enter, passing several signs warning of extreme fire hazard. At what appears to be a cement wall peaking through the trees, we stop. I open the door and at my feet are the remains of someone's campfire. John shakes his head with disgust and leads me down an overgrown trail.

"A reporter from the *Fernie Free Press* came out here a couple of weekends ago to get married. People thought she was nuts. Until they got here."

And there, in an opening in the trees stood what, if I hadn't been told otherwise, I could have sworn were the ruins of a cathedral.

Two-storey cement walls, slightly pink in the evening sun, lined with ten-foot timbered windows on all sides. A gabled roof open to the sky. A profusion of fireweed, oxtail daisies, and saskatoons pushing through the cracks in the cement floor. Grates covering a network of underground tunnels.

"This was the boiler house. It's where coal was burned to make electricity for the mines, and for the town of Hosmer. Here, let me show you the other one." We cross the length of the building, go out the back entrance, through a short stretch of woods, and into another, smaller building of similar construction. Trees have taken over here. A few small spruces have pushed through unimaginably small cracks; an aspen bends with the weight of an impressive wasp nest. John points out the angles of light, his earlier training in architecture showing.

In the eighties, he and some friends asked Ottawa for money to turn this place into an interpretive centre. He points out alcoves where particular exhibits were begging to be built, the views someone in a second-floor coffee shop would have. John spent a good many months guiding apparently appreciative bureaucrats and ministers through here. In the end, they all turned him down.

We make to leave and walk back into the first building. I notice that our words, even spoken softly, seem to rest and hum. "This place has beautiful acoustics," I say. "It would be a lovely place for a concert. Or a play." He seems to brighten at the idea; I tell him he can have it if he likes. I also tell him I know why his reporter friend had her wedding out here.

We have one more thing to see before I really have to get back on the road. Up yet another winding trail, past a rather angry family of grouse, we find ourselves at the abandoned Hosmer cemetery. We walk over to Alderson's headstone. *Greater love hath no man than he lay down his life for his friends.* Thankfully, the mines here closed before any major tragedies happened, so there are only a handful of marked graves. The rest of the clearing has been left to wildflowers and the imagination.

On the way out we stop at a railway crossing as an engine with umpteen coal cars roars westward. As we wait for it to pass, we look across the highway at the mountains, and John tells me the next time I'm back, I have to sit right here and wait for the sun to set. If I do this, he says, I'll see how the mountain's silhouette looks like a man riding a horse.

He deposits me back at the hotel where I've parked my car, and we say goodbye. As I drive away, the image that lingers is of the roots of that cottonwood bearing down and through a wall of milled stone, taking it all back.

[xvi]

The rivers stopped flowing. The birds stopped
flying. The trains no longer ran. All the clocks
stopped. Leaves on the trees crawled back inside
their wooden berths. The cattle stopped eating.

The only thing that remained was her own
heart, stubborn as a deaf mule.

part two

[ch. seventeen]

It is 2:21 AM by the clock in this hotel room, the little red numbers taunting and violent. I have been trying to reach Dr. Ján Lietava for several hours now and each time I try, I get a recorded voice telling me that all circuits are busy. The operator is of no help.

I have not written in a year. I can't remember the names and dates and places of this story, and I have no idea what to do with it. I don't know whether it's fact or fiction. I wanted it to be The Story of Immigrant Women's Experience in Early Coal-Mining Canada, but instead I'm turning up only a series of anecdotes. I am flailing about in history. I am chasing ghosts.

Now I am alone in a dark hotel room in some industrial region of Montreal, unsure of the way home. In short, I am having a meltdown. .

Let me back up a little bit. I am in a hotel room in Montreal because my flight from Toronto (and thence to Frankfurt and Vienna) was delayed and I missed my connection. I will not fly out now until the morning. I have not been writing because I started medical school eight months ago, which thus far has not afforded much mental space for anything else. My life has become alien to me.

I am trying to reach Ján Lietava because he is a specialist in internal medicine at Comenius University in Bratislava. Though we are complete strangers, Dr. Lietava has graciously offered to drive the hour to Vienna to pick me up, to let me stay in his apartment in Bratislava, and to spend as much or as little time in the clinic as I like, getting a sense of the medical system in a country unlike Canada.

Now, standing him up as I'm about to do in a little more than three hours, I recall a dream I often have of wandering out onto a cliff, little safe steps taken one at a time, until suddenly I am too far out and I can go neither forward nor back. Inevitably, I wake up from the dream when I realize I can't write myself out of it. I wonder if I should call the whole thing off and catch the next plane back to Newfoundland.

Everything about this story has proven it does not want to be told. Why can't I just leave well enough alone?

A few things have happened while I have been trying to commit the body to memory. Annie Trenamen passed away before I got the chance to meet her. She was the last of the living children of Andrew and Rosalia. On a whim, I hired a professional researcher in BC to go through the provincial archives there to see if there was anything else I might have missed. It seems I had a bit of beginner's luck: there wasn't much else to be had. She did find Andrew's naturalization records, from January and February of 1906, in the County Court of East Kootenay in Fernie. And in the August 31, 1906 issue of *The Fernie Free Press*, among news of illnesses from typhoid fever, deaths from cholera, and a curious thing called "summer complaint," visits to town by dignitaries, as well as events to watch out for, she found this pitiable notice:

> The two weeks' old child of Mr. and Mrs. Andy Zack,
> a Slav family, died on Monday night. The funeral was held
> from the Roman Catholic church on Wednesday, the services
> being conducted by Father Meissner.

Baby Helen the first.

Lately, I have been reading research about the use of writing as patient therapy. The advice one doctor gives her patients is this: *Start writing from where you are. Start in the middle.*

Yes: the complicated, smelly, clamouring middle, where every day begins and ends.

[xvii]

Once again the blood stops. Though the inside,
outside, and upside-down of her is still raw,
some time during the night of her despair, another
possibility began.

    Babies die. That is the cold steel truth of it.

    And new ones sneak up your skirt when you
least expect it.

[ch. eighteen]

I decide to write myself forward.

After spending the day reading through my notes and getting reacquainted with Rosalia, I am now tucked into my seat on the plane, waiting again for this thing to begin.

I open my bag and take out a few cardiology research papers Dr. Lietava has written — although he's also published papers about mushrooms and the contents of ancient graves, I must remember to ask him about this — and, happily, I am right away thrust into the modern-day reality of the story I am here to research. The per capita income in Slovakia is less than US $10,000, four times less that in neighbouring Austria. Perhaps unsurprisingly, Slovakia's life expectancy is lower. Even its rates of high blood pressure and consequent complications are higher: researchers have often concluded that the health of a population is inversely related to the width of its divide between the rich and poor. Throughout former communist countries of central Europe, the probability of premature death is higher than in western Europe, owing to higher rates of cardiovascular disease (poor diet, alcohol, smoking, stress), accidents, and tuberculosis. These things are especially true for men, particularly unmarried men who feel they lack control over their lives.

Perhaps I am guilty of trying to make everything relevant to everything else, but I can't help but think that getting a glimpse of the most intimate details of people's health concerns will tell me something larger about Slovakia, about its history.

My plane touches down in Frankfurt at 6:30 in the morning local time, just past midnight to my body. Despite pulling a blanket over my head and trying a million different positions, I did not sleep a wink. It is flat here and the air steely. My eyes don't quite work yet, but I can see that the manhole covers are rather artful. As a shuttle bus delivers us across the tarmac to the terminal, I catch myself thinking, "Good God. Why am I here?"

And almost immediately I am thinking, "What if I'd never come?"

Inside the terminal, things are very silver and smooth, all big windows and marble. Past passport control is a long tunnel — the better part of half a mile — outfitted with subtly placed coloured lights that change with the emotional tone of electronica coming from the speakers. There are no windows, no ads that I recall, just two oppositely moving sidewalks and a gangplank down the middle, one long experiential portal. Leave it to the Germans. The paper towels in the bathroom are green and airport employees ride bicycles in the halls. So many parallel worlds on this one perfect planet.

I do not expect Dr. Lietava to be here, on this second day of my arrival, but as I come through the doors from the luggage claim, I cast a glance around the crowd, searching for my name printed on a piece of paper. I see no one, and am slightly relieved that I have not inconvenienced him again. I buy some cash, then head to the bathroom to freshen up. I figure I will catch a bus to Bratislava and call him from there. Then I hear my name over the intercom.

You've got to be kidding.

I rush out to find the information booth, and there I find a tall black-haired man in jeans and shirt sleeves. He shakes my hand, picks up one of my bags, and walks me out to his car.

I recounted to Ján my horror at not being able to reach him. "I had wondered what happened to you. I stayed in the airport three hours. I waited for all the connections from Canada. I thought maybe your flight was cancelled because of what happened in London." Earlier in the week, a group claiming connections with Al-Qaeda had bombed the London Underground, killing dozens, injuring hundreds, and stirring up the anti-terrorism rhetoric once again. "We're next on the list you know. We have five hundred soldiers in Iraq."

He opens the trunk of his Skoda to throw in my suitcase. I ask him if he's been camping. "No. We have study patients all over the countryside. I have to be ready to sleep in my car, if necessary."

On the way to Bratislava, I mention that I'd searched his name in the scientific literature to find him published on all kinds of topics. He chuckles.

"Before studying medicine, I studied history and archaeology. I still teach in archaeology."

I couldn't have found a better host for this trip if I'd tried.

Ján gives me a rolling commentary on centuries' worth of battles and languages and rulers and conquests, which all took place on this soil. "Did you see *The Gladiator?*" he asks.

"Yes," I reply sheepishly. According to the guy at the place where I rent my movies, shootin'-stabbin'-killin' isn't really my thing. I expect him to tell me it was filmed here.

"It took place here. This was part of the Roman Empire. Around this corner you will see the remains of an old fort."

And there it is, poking out of a farmer's field in strange juxtaposition to a nearby cluster of huge white windmills. To a prairie kid like me, one hundred years is a long time. Roman ruins in a farmer's field is something else entirely.

The highway is flat and fast, and in the succession of villages we've driven through, the streets have been tidy and the plaster on the houses freshly painted. After a time, I ask if we're in Slovakia yet.

"No," he says, "a rapid change in living conditions will tell you that."

Another stretch of empty highway, past fields of sunflowers and wheat, and then, high on a hill, a series of severe-looking high-rise buildings. Bratislava. We pass through the border control fairly quickly, and instead of taking the straight route back to his place, Ján decides to give me a brief tour of the old city.

Separating Bratislava Castle from the coronation cathedral, where, for two centuries, the reigning Austro-Hungarian emperor was crowned, is the main highway and a futuristic bridge. Ján tells me that the old Jewish part of town was destroyed in order to put up the bridge, and the traffic on it now rattles the very stones of the cathedral. Beyond this is more in the way of odd pairings: graceful stone buildings with iron balconies and courtyards beside blocky socialist edifices, and garishly painted cow sculptures near where early monuments of the republic were destroyed in favour of offerings to the "mother party." It's an interesting place: part Prague, part Winnipeg. I'm looking forward to exploring on foot.

We pass the military hospital where Ján's wife, Slávka, a rehabilitation physician, works. I ask him about the general state of the medical system here.

"Terrible. Do you know how much a doctor makes?"

"No."

"Guess."

"I don't know."

"Six thousand Canadian dollars per year. And you have seen the prices here."

"How do people make it on that?"

"I don't know." And he left it at that.

On the way back to his family's house for lunch, Ján drives by their apartment, where I am to stay. Last Christmas, they moved into a new home — still under construction, as properly built brick houses can take up to two years to cure — but kept this apartment anyway. It is a large socialist-era concrete block. He gives me a set of keys and we enter a darkened lobby and push the button for the lift. Through the metal door and into the tiny box bedecked with graffiti, lit by one incandescent bulb, we close the door behind us and push the ninth-floor button. The lift starts upward with a jolt and the wall starts sliding away in front of us. We sail past one door, past the thickness of concrete that is the floor, past another door, another floor — it is all mesmerizing to a lift virgin such as myself. Then, at the ninth floor, we stop with a sudden bang and I wonder if something has gone wrong. But no, it is just the door unlocking, and perhaps my jetlagged nerves. He shows me around the apartment — a bedroom, a bathroom, a kitchen, a big fat couch in the living room — what more could I ask?

Home, then, for lunch. On the way, he asks me if I drink alcohol.

"In moderation, I guess."

"What is moderation? Moderation Slovak-style or Canadian-style?"

"Uh — "

"When my grandfather was working, he would drink one litre of *slivovica* per day. And I never saw him drunk." I'm not sure what *slivovica* is, but I tell him my moderation must be of the Canadian kind.

Fittingly, then, seated at his living room table, we start with *slivovica* — which turns out to be plum brandy — served in crystal glasses of the Moravian tradition. It tastes like something that, at the best of times, could do serious damage to one's sense of gravity. I decide to approach it carefully. Then comes *bryndzové halušky* — a traditional stick-to-your-ribs kind of Slovak meal prepared from a sharp, soft sheep's cheese, potatoes boiled with flour, and bacon. This is followed by Moravian wine and so many more dishes of food that I stop counting. Ján and Slávka's daughter, Mirka, and I talk over lunch about her plans to do a year of genetics in university, then follow in her parents' footsteps and go to medical school. After lunch, she shows me her pet rabbit and teaches me a few survival words in Slovak.

At which point it is time for another road trip. The four of us load into the car to go see a castle some fifty kilometres away. On the way, we pass through small villages with houses set close together to preserve land for farming and to protect against the constant string of attacks throughout history that Ján has described. The houses are long, squat brick and plaster affairs, some with small crosses cut into the attic walls, which Ján says are to protect the house. The hardwood forest beyond is deep and dark, with vines covering every surface, yet with a clear understorey, as though green might once have filled the air, but has since settled into a lush mat. There are maples, willows, poplars, dogwoods. A person could be forgiven for confusing it with southern Ontario. Emigrants from here must have been thrilled, if a little surprised, to find that despite the ocean between them, Slovakia and Canada look an awful lot alike. Except for the castles.

At the top of the hill, a security guard stops us and tells us the road is about to be closed for a car race. "Even the president will race in it," Ján reports. He backs up and points the car back down the hill. Not to worry, there are plenty more castles where that one came from. We'll just go to Devín instead.

Devín Castle can set the mind of one not trained in archaeological metrics to spinning. As near as anyone can tell, people have been living here on this hilltop at the confluence of the Danube and Morava Rivers for twenty-six centuries. It started in the fifth century BCE with the Celts, continued in the first century AD with the Romans, and finally became a proper castle in the thirteenth century. Napoleon brought it to its knees in 1809, but mere decades later it was returned to cultural prominence by Ľudovít Štúr, one of the leading figures of the Slovak nationalist movement, whom I had read about before. Štúr would go there to hold revival-type bonfires and poetry readings.

"Language is the closest thing to define Slovaks as a people," Ján explains on the long walk to the top of the ruins. "Štúr chose a Slovak dialect and made it common. Until then, educated people were not speaking the language. They were speaking German, Hungarian, and Latin."

But if no one was speaking it, how was there a dialect to choose?

"The priests spoke Slovak. It was the language people would hear at mass."

Below us, roosters call from their courtyard perches and wild plums ripen on the trees. The Danube and Morava tumble over each other, both swollen from all the rain this summer. Ján points out another ridge in the distance, barely visible, and tells me it is an old road built by the Romans.

What a thing, this lineage. At first, I think, "How could you help but be fiercely proud of such a long and intricate story as this?"

And then I think, "Is it possible to feel smothered by history?"

[xviii]

*This time there is help, and he is sent away to ·
keep him from being underfoot.*

*When he returns, the baby is warm and pink
and her mother's body, in sleep, is unremembering
the pain. The kerchiefed midwife smells of sweat
and coal. She puts the tiny, squirming thing in
his arms.*

Daughter, there is so much to live for.

*And she does. She is the first of whomever will
follow.*

[ch. nineteen]

Eight hours of something closer to death than sleep and I wake up not completely clear of planes and heavy bags, but almost. It is six in the morning and Ján will be calling for me very soon. I go to the kitchen to boil a pot of water for tea (is that fog outside or smoke?), then take a tiny, squatting shower in the bathtub, using a shower-head on a hose running from a hydra-like contraption that also feeds a large sink and a washing machine. I breakfast at the small kitchen table. The room looks out over the back of the apartment building onto a high forested hill. I listen to the building wake up around me.

Ján picks me up before seven and takes me to the clinic. As we approach a long, yellow building tattooed with graffiti, he says, "One hundred years ago, this was the most modern institute in the empire. What you see is the result of privatization. [The government] wants these grounds for development, so they are trying to press us into bankruptcy."

We take a lift up two floors and enter a dark hallway. Ján fiddles with a lock and suddenly we are surrounded by white: white walls, white lights, people in very white linens. He takes a few minutes to change into his own white uniform and whisks us away to the morning meeting.

The meeting is in the library, where hand-bound papers are stored behind glass. There is a ladder for getting at those hard-to-reach letters of the alphabet. White lace curtains billow in front of large open windows. Students, interns, and professors are as-sembled for an update on what happened overnight. From time to time, voices are drowned out by passing streetcars. Ján asks me to introduce myself.

I lean forward in my seat. "Hello. I'm a medical student from Canada. My name is Monica Kidd, and I don't know a word of Slo-vak." A few people smile, a few people do not. The assignments are given and people scatter. I sit in my chair, fingering my stethoscope, waiting for someone to tell me what to do.

It's not long before I realize that not knowing Slovak is going to be a major hurdle for my clinical experience here. The doctors speak English, as do some of the students, but in this environment, slowing to translate is like sprinting in porridge. Since the words I hear mean nothing to me, and I don't even really know where I am, I spend most of the day just watching the comings and goings.

Ján has offered to drive me home from work. Along the way he decides to take a detour to a used bookstore, to see if we can find me some more history books on Slovakia, written in English.

I have a whole sheet full of questions to ask him and figure this is as good a time as any. First, I want to know about land ownership, about this business of Andrew's grandmother growing plums, and the story that one of the reasons Andrew decided to leave Slovakia was that there was no land for him to farm.

"Land has always been privately owned in Slovakia, even during the age of co-operative farms under the communists. In fact, it was better protected under the communists, because it wasn't allowed to be sold for development. If someone stole some trees from some land, the police went and found who it was. Now, nothing."

"And the plums? Was Andrew's grandmother growing the plums for brandy?"

"Probably. Plum brandy has always been very strong in our country, as I have told you. That is one thing. The other thing is, anyone with seven plum trees could ask to be a nobleman. That was a joke in Slovakia, but I have heard it so much there must be truth to it. You must understand that land was everything. After World War I, a guy in south Slovakia who owned a single piece of iron was considered to be rich. There were thousands of people who really had nothing. No job, nothing. There was regular starvation."

"Why was there starvation, if people had land?"

"But they didn't. It was feudalism here. The land was owned by the Hungarian nobility. It was only during the war that feudalism was abolished. The state took all the land."

"How long has land been owned by ethnic Slovaks, then? Only since the middle of the nineteenth century?" I had read that

Ferdinand the Fifth abolished serfdom in 1848, largely in response to the protests of Štúr, but it hadn't occurred to me that this might imply that Andrew's grandmother's ownership of land to grow plums was a recent thing for their family. With my ignorance of all things Slovak and Ján's understandable anger at the state of things in his country — of which he is otherwise proud — it all seems impossibly difficult to understand.

I am also curious about the animosity between Slovaks and Hungarians, both in my grandmother's day and now. I had understood that tendency in my grandparents as their response to historical repression, but this seems incongruous: why would a family who one might think had tried to outrun the past — or, perhaps more properly, the present — by setting up a new life across the ocean and forgetting their language, also decide to drag along old hostilities?

"The Hungarians beat us in the eleventh century," Ján begins. "They suppressed our language and Slovaks hated them for this. We have always been an international family, so to my mind it is irrational, but it is so."

"You mean, my grandfather wouldn't lend a saddle to a Hungarian because of what happened in the eleventh century?" Talk about your grudges.

"Not really. During the Slovak uprising of 1848, we co-operated with Austria in order to defeat Hungary. And we did. But in 1867, Austria and Hungary united and they became equal, and things became very bad for Slovakia." This was when the "Magyarization" I had read about began. Pressburg was re-christened Bratislava, "the glory of brothers." Ján tells me the Slovak national movement made one more break for it with a national uprising in 1944, but the uprising was soon crushed by the Nazis. Thousands were killed, including members of Ján's family. After that it was the communists and their cement. (Here, he interrupted himself to point out the small windows in the newer buildings. They are small because they were built during the Communist era and there is frost in Siberia: by default, then, all Soviet buildings were built for frost, even if it would seem to get hot enough here to melt paint.) After the communists came the Velvet Revolution, when Slovakia wobbled on its own weak legs out onto the dance floor with capitalism. Poor Slovakia, with ornery houseguests coming and going throughout the centuries, and never enough time to mop up between them.

The bookstore is a wonder. I feel certain that no one before in the history of the world has ever managed to cram so many books into two tiny rooms. I wonder if the floor joists might give way. Ján looks for a book illustrated by a particular Slovak painter; I look for anything in English, preferably some local fiction or poetry. I come away with a guide to the museums of Slovakia written eleven years ago.

Back in the car, I resume my cross-examination. "What about school? Andrew left school when he was fourteen. Was that normal?"

"Six years of school was obligatory in the cities, but in the villages, children went to school for as long as their parents could afford. They started when they were six years of age." And yes, the girls went to school, too. What about this business of him walking from town to town, selling glass?

"Ah, he was a drotár. That was typical for that part of the country. These people repaired pottery with iron wires. Do you remember those things we saw for sale?" At Devín, we had seen a man at a kiosk selling trinkets he made from twisted wire. "That's what your great-grandfather did."

"Hard work," I say.

"It wasn't work, it was an attempt to survive. They were seen as poor people with enterprise. According to the communists, they were the best example of the exploitation of workers. You know, it wasn't simply that if you were clever you could make something for yourself, as in Canada, in Alberta. Here, every metre of land belonged to someone for centuries. It was broken up into very small pieces over the years. Land here is the most important thing in the world."

As it remains for my family.

"How would he have saved up enough money to get across the Atlantic?"

"They would borrow the money. There was a term for it: *chief carte*. It would take them six to nine months to pay back."

So many questions. From whom did they borrow? How often did people default? What happened when they did? I try to contain myself because our car trip is drawing to a close, and there are only so many questions the average set of ears can tolerate in one afternoon.

"It's funny, you know. Andrew went to selling glass because he swore up and down he would never go to the mines. Then he travelled halfway around the world and found himself in the mines."

"Well, let's just say it was better paid in Canada. And you know, if you are living at home you are ashamed to do certain things in front of people. But when you are away, you do what you need to survive."

What about the arts? Why have I never heard of any Slovak writers or painters? Why has it been so hard for me in Canada to read the story of Slovakia as told and shown by Slovaks?

"There are artists, but they don't declare themselves as Slovaks. Have you ever heard of Andy Warhol? He was a Slovak. But our greatest painter is Husarik. And our greatest poet was Hviezdoslav. It means 'one who is speaking about the stars.' He was Hungarian. He was writing after World War I. You must understand that Slovaks were always the poor man, and this is also in culture." Later, I learn Hviezdoslav was a pen name, that he lived in the district of Orava (Andrew and Rosalia's birthplaces are also in Orava), and that his work relies heavily on words and expressions he invented, making them difficult to translate into English. Which seems ironic, since his day job was translating other works into Slovak.

"You must understand that Slovaks want leaders. Many of the intelligentsia left before the Russian Revolution in 1917. We were rich in the 1930s. We were not hit as hard as America during the Depression. I never starved. But somewhere deep in our parents is the fear of hunger. Yet we were well educated and there was much industry. You know this Jánošík?"

"The Robin Hood guy?"

"Yes. There has also been an attitude of cut and run here. Maybe that is why there is not more art. But we produce a lot of good hockey players."

I come home from the day tired and famished, tear open the rest of a pack of chocolate cookies on the windowsill and devour them. I plug in my computer to charge, using a converter Ján has just taken me to a shopping mall to buy. Happily, it doesn't explode. Then I make myself a bit of supper and drag my lazy limbs out for a run. I'm not sure where to go so I keep to the residential areas — new brick houses with high fences and voluptuous gardens alongside socialist-era apartments dressed in spray paint — and everywhere, puddles from the day's sudden storm. Eventually, I find myself in a field, and I am running through the long grass and slimy mud, trying (and failing) to avoid entire civilizations of snails beneath my sneakers, looking out over the misty hills, knowing my mother would die a thousand deaths if she knew I was running by myself in a partly forested empty lot with no identification in a place where I can't speak the language, until I arrive in a lavish gated yard, complete with rock gardens and tennis courts. I turn back and run home along the highway and share a ride up in the lift. Together we watch the layer cake of the building go by. He is as startled by the *clack* of the opening lock as I am.

[xix]

She digs a hole in the woods behind the house.
She finds a barrel and lines it with an old sheet.
She retrieves the red coat, which is hanging in the
house, innocent of all crimes. She folds it, places
it in the barrel, and closes the lid. She lowers the
barrel into the ground. She picks up the shovel
and covers the barrel with rich, black soil.

It will be there if she ever needs it, which she
won't, but in the meantime she's had enough of
its incessant whispering, and besides, there's
another baby on the way.

So.

[ch. twenty]

On our way into work, Ján and I stop at one of the city's four other hospitals. This hospital is as good as, or perhaps better than, a Canadian hospital, with bright, cheery corridors, framed drawings by children, and patients wandering in handsome institutional pyjamas. In a study of contrasts, we head straight back down to the University hospital. We take the creaky lift and step into the dark hallway, but this time we are locked out because the lock has given up. Ján uses his cellphone to call someone to let us in.

Because I don't speak the language, and because I'm so early in my training, I'm more of an anthropologist than a participant on this mission to the clinic. I am impressed with the soft musicality of people's voices. People have a calm, level way of dealing with each other. There is a sense of shared work, even among the patients, who quite readily strip down to their skivvies or less in front of whomever might happen to be dressed in white.

Up on the wards, the large, open windows look out over the broken rooftops of the Bratislava. Soft pre-rain air sniffs down the hallway as a stooped old soul shuffles off to use the bathroom. For certain, there is less money in this hospital than what I am used to. But here, under the cut-glass lampshades of the incandescent lights — every other one unlit — and through the door into the patients' room where small tables stand covered with tablecloths for civilized meals, I also think there is something very much more.

After the clinic, Ján walks with me out to the old city. I've decided to take the afternoon to poke about. He buys me a deep-fried snack, something like a Pogo stick but filled with a sweet poppy paste, then sends me on my way. I look for a museum of emigration, and find that it has been turned into a hospital. I wander the side streets, wanting to be away from the constant rush of traffic. The houses here are three storeys of brick and plaster, with small balconies, each with their own explosions of flowers. And there are the gargoyles I so love, grimy from the industrial stacks that dot the horizon. To whom did these faces once belong? Who is admired here? Who is forever mocked?

The main courtyard of Bratislava Castle offers a commanding and sobering view of the city. To the south of the Danube, the city is heart-stopping uniformity, seeming to summon an efficiency against which the human condition rebels; to the north, it is a wise old woman reclining in a faded daybed, swirling a cognac and watching over her daughter in stilettos. I have no right to feel nostalgia for a time when this place was free of huge billboards advertising Coca-Cola, but I do.

The castle houses the national museum, which contains artifacts spanning an incomprehensible distance of the human journey, and they are impressive, without a doubt. But what I'm here to see is the exhibit called "Until the bride said Yes." I note the pomp and wealth represented by brides' trousseaus throughout the ages. Over time the dresses become less like armour and more like nightgowns, then turn back again. I find a dress that women of Rosalia's era wore: high-necked, off-white, with puckered shoulders, ruffles on the hem of the floor-length skirt, and a wreath of greenery heart the waist. Rosemary, perhaps? For memory and virginity?

I never did get a good read on the word "Until."

Back at the apartment, I find a beautiful young woman with long, black hair standing silently behind the door. Mirka (not Ján's daughter, but another) is to be my guide for the rest of my time here. She is a medical student like me, though much further ahead in her training, and is from the city of Dolný Kubín in the district of Orava. She will go to Ottawa in August, and by spending time with me, will get a chance to practice her English. And, as I'll soon come to learn, she'll make the rest of my search possible.

It's been a long day for both of us; she's been to Vienna to get her student VISA and plane ticket in order. After supper and a bit of getting-to-know-you talk, we both turn in. Tomorrow, yet another medical student, Martin, will drive us to northern Slovakia, where they will help me dredge the records for traces of Andrew and Rosalia.

[xx]

When the whistle begins, she is looking in the
mirror thinking that soon she will be an old
woman, her white wiry hair wild in the wind.
Still two hours before the end of his shift. She
bundles the baby and pulls an old sweater
over her girth, whispering No, no, no, no, no.

At the bottom of the hill, the women are not
speaking in all the languages of the world. They
are white with shock. Or they are red with shock.
Another set of greasy, black feet arrives. Another
intake of breath. Another shriek, another swoon.

A hand on her shoulder, and she wheels. It's
not his turn this time.

It's not her turn.

This time.

[ch. twenty-one]

At 5:30 in the morning the sun falls on the cement blocks opposite ours. As we wait for Martin's call, Mirka and I have our breakfast and talk about the place where Rosalia was born, the place where Mirka's family still lives.

"Orava is the poorest region of Slovakia. Here, around Bratislava, they grow all the vegetables they want. In Orava, no. There, in the past, there were just small houses, made of wood, with maybe five, six, ten people."

I tell her Rosalia's tale, about her trip across the Atlantic, then across North America, finally to marry a stranger, a man she'd never met before. I ham it up a little, so she knows how obsessed I've become with the story, and also to try to make myself better understood, working as we are around this big, ugly language barrier.

"You think it is crazy that your great-grandparents never meet before they marry. But it was common. Their parents said, 'This land is close to ours, and you will marry so you will make it bigger.'"

Like Ján said the other day, land was the most important thing. More important than will, more important than love: it meant bread on the table. It meant identity.

With all the talk I'd heard about bad roads in Slovakia, I was beginning to expect little more than a cattle trail north. As we leave behind the city limits of Bratislava, I tell Martin the roads here are as good as any in Canada.

"Oh." He smiles. "Slovaks are not content people."

We pass the factories on the Danube, which flows from here into the Black Sea. We pass billboards and big-box stores too numerous and horrific to mention. We pass fields of sunflowers standing on file in east-facing armies. And storks, apparently off-duty.

We are on our way to Bytča. Despite the linguistic ministrations of my two excellent guides, nothing is going to convince my tongue to do the gymnastics required to say the name properly. They giggle every time I say it. I'm sure there's a reason.

Driving through these small towns, I realize that all the older houses are covered with plaster. I had always thought the stucco obsession of western Canada was an artifact of post-World War II modernity. Now I see that perhaps it rode the coattails of so many central European immigrants. Perhaps it was an attempt to make the flimsy wooden houses of the New World seem substantial.

But I also see that my expectations of small-town Slovakia were completely wrong. These are not tiny villages awash in pastoral splendour — they are that, too, as evidenced by men working their hayfields with scythes under a sun already hot at eight, and their hand-piled haystacks — they are semi-urban places with truck stops and billboards and Volkswagen dealerships and kids with purple hair. The Slovakia of my great-grandparents seems impossibly distant right now. As perhaps it should.

We arrive in Bytča at around nine and get directions to the archives. The archives, I'm delighted to learn, are in a Renaissance castle built by an Italian for the Turso family, one of the richest of its day. We cross a canal on a small footbridge and pass through the gate, where no fewer than three people are sweeping the cobblestones. Through the inside castle wall, then another courtyard and another sweeper. Here, the air is cool. The mezzanine walls were once painted with stories of kings and battles; they are faded now to black and grey. Sections of the plaster have fallen off altogether. We go upstairs to find the office of the archives.

We tell the woman behind the desk who were are — Ján has already made an appointment for us — and she begins to show Mirka the forms we need to fill out. While the two women work out the details, I glance around the room. Stacks of age-yellowed ledgers crowd around a swank new computer screen. The ceiling is braced by giant square-cut beams. There are big windows through which comes the sound of sweeping. Without overhead lights, the room is a little dark, but gentle and civilized, and I — fluorescent-light hater that I am — am in heaven.

The archivist retrieves three boxes of microfiche and leads the three of us to the projector in the corner. She inserts the baptismal records for Trstená around the time of Rosalia's birth, and without pause, scrolls directly to it.

And there is Rosalia. I'm sure my eyes bug. The record headings indicate — in Latin — the date of birth and date of baptism, name of the baby, sex of the baby, whether the baby was legitimate or illegitimate, the address and names of the parents, the names of the godparents and priest, as well as some "For office use only" areas, which were never fully explained to me. Her record indicates that she was, indeed, born on September 1, 1884 and baptized the following day. Her parents, of "335 Trstená," were Johannes Patalla and Veronica Trstenská. Her godparents were Martinus Shurina and Rosalia Fábri. There, at least, is the correct spelling of her name, and proof I'm on the right track. And with her parents' names, we can look for any siblings she might have had.

In goes another microfiche, this one the list of all the babies born in a particular area, by year. Two hours of hunting and gathering follow, but with Mirka at the helm of the microfiche, Martin working the focus bar, and me sitting in dumbfounded amazement at both their generous help and the quality of the information we were finding, we came up with the following picture:

Rosalia was the oldest of seven children born over eleven years. There was Maria, Franciscus, Ignatius (who died two days before his first birthday), the twins Johanna and Helena, and another Helena, born three years later. We ask the archivist about this. She says the twin Helena likely died, and bequeathed her name to the next daughter. An eerie coincidence that Rosalia's first daughter Helen died and that Rosalia also chose to pass along the name. Perhaps the second Helena was lucky, although she likely would not have known. Rosalia's baby sister was only six years old when Rosalia left for Canada. It's now a little easier to see why she left: nothing divided by seven is indeed a small number.

We discover Andrew listed under October 6, 1882, as Andreas Zsiak, with parents Andreas Zsiak and Susana Matay. He was the second-youngest child, with only Stephanus behind him. Before them came Maria, born in 1869 and dead four years later;

Johannes, who died days after his fifth birthday; Maria; Josephus; and a second Johannes. No Christopher, as Ken Zak had recalled. Ken also said Andreas' parents died during an epidemic when he was two years old, but we do not look for these records. Is it possible they both died so soon after little Stephanus was born? Parentless during an epidemic, what chance would there have been for the baby to survive?

So there it is. After so many months of looking, my clearest picture of Andrew (no, Andreas) and Rosalia. I am relieved, as if I've washed up on shore after being adrift at sea.

"It's a pretty town," says Martin.

"Very pretty," I agree. I am inspired to try the name again. "Bytča. Bytča. Byt-ča."

Martin giggles again and says, "I wouldn't say that out loud. It sounds like something else."

"Right. What does it sound like?"

"I'll tell you in the car."

We find a place for lunch and walk back to the car, where we leave the doors open for a few minutes so that our blood won't boil in our veins. It's become breathlessly hot. As soon as we're sitting inside, I ask again what this word is that I apparently keep saying. Mirka says, diplomatically, "It's an insult."

I wait for more, but do not get it. I'm dying to know. As we round the corner and return to the highway, I say to Martin, "You're not going to tell me, are you?"

"It's bad."

"Is it a body part?"

"Yes."

"Male or female?"

"Female."

"Above the waist or below?"

"Below."

Enough said. I roll down my window, which makes it too loud to talk, so we don't.

When Martin drops us off the only thing I want to do is change into my shoes and run. I had tried (and failed) to find the road to Devín on an earlier run. Now that I have a vague map of the neighbourhood in my mind, I figure I'll give it another go. I tell Mirka I'll be back in an hour and take myself back downstairs in the lift.

This time, success! I switchback through the neigbourhood until I find a corner with a sign pointing the way to Devín. I am met with a muddy footpath running a fairly steep pitch up a wooded hillside. It had looked like an actual road on the map. I am dubious. But where I run makes no real difference to me, as long as I do run, so I continue. About a kilometre through what sometimes feels like someone's back yard, I come to a paved road, and soon after that, an intersection. I stop and have a look around. No indication which way I should go.

An old man getting into his car calls out to me a string of words, among which I recognize only one: Hotel?

"No," I say, forgetting what language I'm supposed to be speaking. "Devín?"

He begins to point and presumably explain the way. His friend, a few metres behind him and getting into his own car, joins in. I smile and shrug. "Nie slovensky. Canadian."

"Canadian! Canadian!" He says, understanding. His friend takes over, and begins with more directions. I shrug again.

He is pointing and drawing in the air what I think he means to be a sign. Then he motions for me to follow. A few steps down the road, he laughs and points to his feet. One foot is in a sandal, the other in a hiking boot covered with burrs. He was so eager to help he'd forgotten to finish was he was doing.

He walks me to the trail's entrance and points to a set of signs on a pole, one of which is for Devín. He motions that the Devín signs have a yellow arrow to distinguish them from signs for other trails.

"Ďakujem," I say. Thank you.

He waves as he walks off in his mismatched shoes. "Prosím."

Oh, sweet release of running. And the forest swallows me whole.

Over supper, Mirka and I talk about churches, the coronation cathedral downtown, the beauty of the ceremony. She was baptized only last year; when she was a child, it was illegal under socialism for her mother, a teacher, to baptize her. I tell her I don't follow any religion, but that I appreciate churches for their understanding that beauty and ceremony can elevate the human condition, especially because I find so much of North America ugly, because of its sameness, its disposability.

She tells me about the bells in the tower of the cathedral. Then she is stuck for a word. Her hands form a globe in the air. "What do you call the inside of the bell?"

"The clapper."

"Here, we call it the heart."

[xxi]

The bread is better, but the sheets are not. She
hangs them when she ought, but coal hangs in
the air like oxygen and everything is grey. Surely
she and the babies will follow, chameleon-like.
Wherever in the world they go, they will be
marked. My people, says the Pass.
    Fair trade.
    Give up your guts for the commerce of the
world, and the least you deserve is a Diaspora.

[ch. twenty-two]

This is my last day at the clinic and I still have not spoken to one patient. Mirka volunteers to change that. We go upstairs, speak to the intern in charge of the ward, and let ourselves in.

The first man is a construction worker from eastern Slovakia. He has no family except for a live-in girlfriend. He had come across the country for surgery on his varicose veins, but as the doctors were doing preparatory tests, they discovered he had life-threateningly high blood pressure. They wouldn't operate until they'd brought it down; he has been in hospital for two weeks.

The second man, in a bed two arms' lengths from the first, has lung problems. Doctors weren't sure whether it was cancer or tuberculosis, or just what it might be. All they knew was what the chest x-ray told them: there was something filling up the airspaces, something that ought not to be there. They would take a small sample of the fluid in his lungs and try to find out what it was.

He is riddled with scars, this man. The scar down the middle of his belly and veering around the hairpin curve of his navel is from a bladder reconstruction he had some years ago. The scar on his back is from kidney surgery. His legs don't work; an accident left him a paraplegic. I ask the patients questions about how the medical system works here. Despite the crumbling outward appearance of this noble building, it appears the men are quite happy with the treatment they are receiving. The closeness of the room means they know each other's business, and that seems quite fine by them, too.

Soon, the intern comes and interrupts us to carry out a procedure. But before we go, Mirka tells them about my additional reason for being in Slovakia.

There is much commotion and some laughter.

"They say you are one of ours."

After the clinic, Mirka and I go back to Ján's flat to get our bags, then take the tram downtown again to get the train to Kral'ovany, where we will catch another train to her parents' home in Dolný

Kubín. At the station, I discover my credit card won't work for some reason no one knows. We buy ice cream to mollify my growing traveller's unease: heavy bags, hot feet, uncertainty about how to get around, and the now-physical need to catch up on my writing.

The train is a relief. It is smoother than any I have ever travelled on. The cars are divided into rooms with six seats with head rests and baggage racks that work. I have a little table on which I can fold my arms and watch the landscape roll by. It is a four-hour trip and Mirka dozes while I write. The rain starts and stops. Peaks — to shed the winter's generous snow — appear on the roofs of houses as we head northward, with lightning close behind us.

At Dolný Kubín, we walk across the tracks to the platform where a few people are waiting or coming or going. In the station — lit, like so many public places by ambient light — Mirka goes to speak with the ticket agent about tomorrow's trip. A boy sneaks up behind her and yells "Boo!"

It's Martin, Mirka's little brother, here with a friend to help us carry our bags home.

Up the hill we go to the family flat, where Ján and Melánia, Mirka's parents, are waiting on the balcony. They are smiling and waving.

Inside, Melánia has made pizza for Mirka and me. She gives us each a tall mug of lemon tea while Mirka tells them the story of Andreas and Rosalia. I expect she will soon be more expert in my lineage than I am. I ask questions about land ownership — land was the most important thing, after all — and about Andreas' life as a drotár. Ján becomes excited and explains through Mirka that he is a drotár, too, after a fashion: he works with iron and makes keys, though he doesn't go from town to town as Andreas did, and certainly not on foot.

I want more details, so I explain — through Mirka — about the glass and the big packs. I still wonder whether the feats of these people have not been a little exaggerated.

Ján's expression changes. He speaks to Mirka and taps the window behind him.

"He says that your great-grandfather was not a *drotár*, he was a *sklár*. *Sklárs* worked with glass. *Drotárs* worked with iron and ceramic. People became *sklárs* when they had no land. It was very hard work. They were very strong and could never rest." I ask Mirka to explain about Andreas burying his wallet at night so as not to be robbed, and her father nods. "Exactly," the gesture says.

When I begin asking about history, it's Martin's turn to jump in with answers. His father begins, but Martin, with his sparkling brown eyes, finishes. Pretty impressive, I think, for a fifteen-year-old kid otherwise into computer games and hockey. We all lament — again — about our language barrier, but with the tireless work of Mirka we seem to be making out okay. Ján hunches up his shoulders to say that Czechs were always strong and in power; he slides his hand out low to indicate that Slovaks were the small man.

Because they are curious, I tell them about the farming my family does and how cold it gets in winter. I tell them my mother called last winter on a day that, with the wind chill, was minus 55 degrees. I tell them about the winter in the 1950s that was so cold Sid Hepburn's cows froze to death standing in the fields and didn't fall over until the spring came and their legs thawed. They laugh, perhaps because I myself am laughing so hard that my eyes are watering. (I'm sure poor old Sid didn't find it so funny.) I ask them if they ever hear anything about Canada here in Slovakia. Martin says, "NHL." He's a Habs fan.

We move out into the living room and talk about plans for tomorrow's trip to Trstená. I'm not sure what I can, or want, to find out, but I would like to get a sense of where the Patallas lived, and we have a few of their street numbers from the *matrika*. I expect the family home will have been bulldozed for a Wal-Mart or something, but even if I can stand in the general area and look around, I'll consider my trip a success. I wonder if there is a museum or some such place where old town maps might be archived. Ján and Melánia recommend asking at the town office, then going on to the *matrika*.

I ask about Kvačany. They've never heard of it. Maybe it is under Orava Lake? Perhaps, I say, but we did find a village that is a likely candidate on an atlas in the clinic, and it looks to be not so far from here. They find their own atlas and I point it out. "It is a very small village," Mirka says. "Look on the map. Each of these grey dots is a house. There are what, less than thirty?"

I ask about getting there — on the bus or train, or maybe I can rent a car? They talk for a while between themselves. Then Mirka says, "If you stay for Saturday, my family's car will be fixed and Daddy says he will drive you."

Oh no. Did my curiosity sound like a demand? I feel that I've made a blunder, and try, unsuccessfully, to explain. "We will see tomorrow," says Mirka. Conversation turns to what I've seen and done so far in Slovakia. They are pleased to hear that I like *bryndzové halušky*, the sheep's cheese I had at Ján Lietava's, and say it must be my Slovak roots. Then they ask me about something for which Mirka can't find the word. Melánia takes me to the kitchen, pulls out a pot of soup from the fridge and fishes for something with a spoon.

Sauerkraut. I nod appreciatively and try to explain to her with hand gestures about the sauerkraut rolls my mom makes. I tell her about the *pirožky* we make (although mine are a little pathetic). We all have a shot of vodka then, and it's time for bed. Mirka tells me her mom says that if I stay another night, she'll make the sauerkraut soup for supper.

Melánia makes a bed for me on the pull-out couch in the living room. When everyone has retired, I pick up the phone book and search for Patallas. Not a single one, in all of northern Slovakia.

[xxii]

She is tired. A baby on her hip. Another at
her side drawing circles with the toe of her
shoe. Two brown-haired beauties with eyes
the colour of cloth.

They are standing in the butcher's. Baby
Number One needs to pee. Baby Number
Two is starting the long, slow approach to
an inconsolable howl. She cannot, for the
life of her, remember the word Pig. She
wants to go home.

But she can't remember that, either.

[ch. twenty-three]

Mirka wakes me up at six AM. Two cups, one of tea and the other of coffee, wait for me on the kitchen table. I drop them both into my gullet and we rush to get ready. For a moment I stand in front of the hallway mirror. After a week of wear, my rumpled sweater and shorts look like they could fit two of me. I should feel ashamed of myself. But I do not. Instead, ready to step out with my new friend, I feel very much the Victorian lady traveller, a girl on a driving trip to the country. I should have a scarf around my hair, perhaps some hosiery. I should be using words like "charming" and "besotted."

It is foggy this morning. We rush down the hill to the train station and make it with exactly one minute to spare. The train plods its way north and west. The tracks are so overgrown that tree branches brush the windows. The Orava River is swollen and brown. The high sedimentary cliffs are topped with impossibly tall spruce and dotted with stubborn patches of flowers. Between stretches of cliffs lie fields full of potatoes and cabbage and garlic, poppy flowers standing tall as schoolboys. *Land is the most important thing.* Dirt paths wander off into the woods.

How badly Rosalia and Andrew must have wanted this for themselves.

The man across from me is moving his lips ever so slightly. A string of rosary beads slips between his thumb and fingers. The sky clears to the clearest blue. These things I understand better than breathing.

Here is where I should say that I was adopted. Rosalia is my great-grandmother by arrangement, not blood. But genetics has nothing to do with the power this land holds over me, just as it has for anyone who has ever longed for a piece of earth. Without Rosalia, my own life would not have unfolded the way it has. Without this land, there would have been no Rosalia. Therefore, I choose to call this my own. *She's one of ours.*

What's so special about this place? Nothing. Everything.

At 8:15, we reach the edge of town. To the west is a forested hill. To the east, a field. To the south, a man sitting in a chair watching over his goats.

When we step out of the station, tinny folk music from loud-speakers wired to light poles greets our ears. There is a small fair in town today, which we will check out once we've done our business at the *matrika*. We wander down the street and pass two boys squatting in the dirt, playing war with an anthill. A stork stands in its rooftop nest and flaps its wings. Street signs point the way to Krakow.

The woman in the *matrika*, with her red pantsuit and carefully pencilled eyebrows, is the emblem of efficiency. She tells us no early maps of the town exist and is ready to return to her desk when we assault her with our list of further questions. She disappears into the back room in search of Johanna Patalla, the twin born in 1892 who survived and married Josepho Kudlicka at the old-for-then age of thirty-five. We had discovered this in Bytča.

After some time and a bit of muttering, she reemerges to say she has searched the birth records from the date of marriage up until the 1950s and there are no records of any children. We ask if we might have a look just in case. She returns with a large yellowed ledger with a green-striped cover. We search through all the Ks for thirty years and nothing. That makes it easy. And maybe not so strange, given the fact that she married so late. That is the more interesting mystery. How about baby Helena?

Again, more time passes — the woman helping us also has to serve other people who appear. From time to time we stand to the side and wait.

This time, she appears with good news. On January 30, 1919, at the age of twenty-four, Helena Patalla married Stephano Jankola, a man two years her junior. But again, the *matrika* contains no record of children. There are no records of any description for the elder children, Maria and Franciscus. Rosalia, of course, went to Canada, and Ignatius perished in his first year.

This may explain why there are no Patallas in the phone book.

According to what we've learned this morning, the Patalla-Trstensky family line died out in Slovakia in its first generation.

After a tour through the fair in the town square (where I buy a *pirožky press* and a small painting of the church for my mother), Mirka and I stop for lunch and afterwards wander about. Even without maps, I still wonder if we might find where the Patallas used to live: people's memories can often astound.

The cries of roosters blend with the music still blaring from the light poles. In the older part of town, we notice that houses have two numbers. We start counting up from around 200. The *matrika* in Bytča listed Johannes and Veronica as living in 313, 315, and 335 over their child-bearing years. We follow the numbers around corners until we find where 335 ought to have been: if it ever existed, it's now a barn. The numbers 313 and 315 are both modern houses. And we don't even know if these numbers correspond to the ones in the *matrika*.

We stop to speak to a woman standing in the street and ask her if she knows anything about this dual numbering system. She doesn't, but as we're about to continue on our way, a woman passing on a bicycle and stops. Mirka tells her who we are and there are a few minutes of talking before Mirka lets me in on it, whispering, "She knew the Patallas."

The Tom Stoppard play *Rosengrantz and Gildenstern Are Dead* opens with Rosengrantz flipping a coin and turning up an absurd number of heads in a row. Pondering this, he says, "Consider. One — probability is a factor which operates within natural forces. Two — probability is not operating as a factor. Three — we are now held within un-, sub-, or super-natural forces. Discuss!" Having, on the second try, encountered someone who knew a family that has not lived in the area since before I was born seems absurdly lucky to me. Call me Rosencrantz.

The woman and Mirka continue talking until Mirka says goodbye and we carry on: our train leaves in ten minutes.

"People here were only farmers," she begins. By "only" she means farming was the only occupation in town. "Not really farmers. They were rol'níks, from rol'a, which means 'field.' If you had no field, you had no food. They were rich because they didn't need to buy food. Sometimes, when there was extra, they would sell, and they would have money. She remembers her father talking about the Patallas, and she said she was glad because there have been no people with that name here for forty years. Her brother has the nickname Palo Patalla because in Slovak it rhymes with pig killer." Charming.

"The numbers here have been changed twice, so that what was 315 one hundred years ago is now 415. You understand?"

We have no time to go back and find the precise houses, but we have just come from walking along the road where they would likely be. The street lies between the town square and where the train track now runs; Rosalia was two years old when it was built. In a moment, it carries us out of town.

I have decided to stay for Saturday and Melánia, as promised, sets a bowl of the sauerkraut soup in front of me seconds after I sit down at the kitchen table. This is followed by pirožky. They're going to have to roll me out of here.

After supper I head out for a solitary walk. It is perfectly still and warm, even though the sun is on its way to setting and we are surrounded by mountain peaks. I trudge across an open field in platform sandals and pass a group of people sitting at a fire and toasting marshmallows. Looking down to watch where I'm going, I find a four-leaf clover. I walk to the top of the hill to see into the next valley. On the way back, I cut back through a field of wildflowers so tall they reach my waist. And to think I almost decided not to come.

Tomorrow, Kvačany.

[xxiii]

She writes the words Dear Mother on the top of
page and sets down the pencil. A grandmother
would want to know when she becomes one, but it
has been so long and there are not enough words
in her head to tell all that has happened.

It has been a long time. Am I a stranger to you?

No. She throws the paper in the stove and begins again.

Dear Mother.

˹[ch. twenty-four]

I try to at least pay for the gas but Ján won't let me. "You are the guest, you do not pay," Mirka explains. "He will be glad to take you. He wants to show you the beautiful places." We pile our things — bags, binoculars, a cooler full of food — into the Skoda, and we're off. The forecast had been for rain. Fortunately, the forecast is wrong.

Mirka has seen me wildly snapping photos from the train windows and in Trstená, and has given her father appropriate warning. "When you want to take a picture, say. We will stop."

I'm fond of the haystacks so we stop at a field with an army of them. I scrabble up the bank and muck around in the wet field a while until I am humbled by the task of trying to capture its expanse. As I settle for an adequate shot, I hear a haunting percussive melody roll out of the hills. It reminds me of something. I look up and around, and there, on the top of a hill across the road is a herd of about one hundred cattle. Cowbells. A whole chorus of them.

I use my zoom lens to get a better look, and silhouetted on the ridge are three men, walking among the cattle, driving them. I cut back across the field and Ján offers me a hand as I step back down into the ditch.

I had developed a blister underneath the strap of my sandal the day before, and now my walk in the sodden field has rubbed it raw. I could suffer through it, but I ask if there might be any tape in the car, or whether we could stop at a store where I could buy some bandages. We check the first-aid kit in the car, but no luck. He says we will stop at his friend's house in Málatiná; hopefully, he will be home.

Ján Martinovič lays down the scythe with which he was cutting his front lawn and takes us to the medicine cabinet in the dining room. He sets out boxes and boxes of bandages for our perusal, along with a small bottle of antiseptic spray. He lifts a small jar containing something that resembles sauerkraut, then returns it to the shelf.

"What's that?" I ask.

"This is a plant that helps healing. You want to try it?"

"Can I?"

Ján returns with scissors and Mirka sits me down in a chair. She cuts a width of bandage from the long strip and a small piece of the plant. I smell the bottle. Vodka.

She hands me a slip of the plant and motions for me to put it on my blister, now open and angrily red. It stings as Mirka tapes the bandage in place. And then the pain is gone.

"What is the plant?"

She can't remember its name in English and consults her father.

"It's this mark of the French."

"Fleur-de-lys?"

"Yes. It is lily."

The two Jáns are talking loudly. I hear the word "Canada" and immediately, Ján Martinovič is assembling the bottles of hospitality. Mirka and Ján are telling him no and gesturing with smiles: seeing as how it's just after eight in the morning, maybe the slivovica can wait for another day.

Outside, Ján is checking his directions with his friend, and I am starting to recognize just enough words to know they are discussing my family and the reason for our journey. "He says the railway was built in 1886," Mirka tells me. I am surprised he knows the precise date. "He works in the matrika." Well, then. I start in with my battery of questions.

"Your great-grandfather would have borrowed money from family and people around. Or he would have worked on the ship. Many people did this." Ján speaks for a bit longer. "He would have walked through Poland to get to Hamburg."

"And the sklárs?" Mirka smiles. I must seem obsessed about this.

At this, he becomes even more animated, something I would have thought impossible. He hunches up his shoulders, as though carrying a heavy pack; he waves his arms as though drawing invisible lines around an empire. "The sklárs were famous throughout Europe. There were many from this region. We will be passing a town, Vel'ké Borové, where only sklárs lived, because it was very cheap. They were all of the *sklárs* from Slovakia. Each had his own territory."

Never have I been so grateful for a blister.

We leave town on a one-lane gravel road winding through tall forest and taller cliffs. Then it's out past a lake called Liptovská Mara, where we take a brief wrong turn and see a dozen men in Speedos and life jackets pulling a trailer with a motorboat up a steep hill to the main road: many Slovaks and foreigners come here to vacation. We right ourselves and come out onto a broad plain full of fields and sunshine. Another grand old church appears around another bend, and with it, a sign declaring "Kvačany 3 KM."

It's just after nine o'clock, and the farmers are bent at their fields. There are the usual potatoes and poppies and plots of grass. I ask the purpose of the plastic pop bottles hanging from lines in the fields. "To scare the birds," Mirka says. In Newfoundland, it's plastic grocery bags. Never underestimate the skittishness of birds and the inventiveness of farmers.

We park at the bus station and start walking toward the church tower. We stop where two men are giving their lawn the once-over with scythes. At the mention of history, the younger man defers to the older, whose smile appears glued to his face. He wears a cardigan and a jaunty engineer-style cap.

Mirka begins to smile. "He says he knew the Zsiaks. They lived in that house there, the second one with the red roof." I stare, not quite able to believe what I've just heard. "It was Josephus Zsiak who lived there. He was Andreas' brother, yes?"

I consult my book. Mirka has come to know these people better than me. Josephus was indeed Andreas' brother. The old man waves to a man working across the street. Mirka and her father explain who we are and what we are up to. He looks at me while he speaks to Mirka. There are rapid-fire exchanges, then he disappears across the road, taking with him a plastic bag and an axe.

"That was the mayor of the town. He had to go. He says the church was built in the fourteenth century. He says Josephus was an important man here. He was mayor in the 1930s and 1940s, I don't know when. And also, he was this man who wears a black robe, who knows what is wrong and right." A judge? "Yes, a judge."

We are causing quite a stir. Another man approaches us from across the street. He, too, is wearing a cardigan and a jaunty cap. He is small and his old back is bent nearly double. Judging from his hands, his infirmity is from a life of hard work. With a smile, he tells us that he is the worst man in town, and invites us back to his house for coffee.

After a few sentences, Mirka says, "Josephus was this man's godfather." Just to make sure we're talking about the same Josephus Zsiak, I ask if he died in 1944. Indeed, he had. After so many dusty alleys down which this search has lead me, sitting here at this table in this village — three hundred souls, I am later told — on this sunny Saturday morning seems utterly unreal. Rosencrantz, Rosencrantz, Rosencrantz.

The discussion he and Mirka and Ján have is an animated one. I am busting to know what they're saying. Mirka is taking notes and smiling, so it must be good. She whispers, "I'll tell you later."

Ladislav Klepáč's eighty-eight years show in the prominent bones on his face. He is shiny and bronzed from years under the sun. Though I am warm in my shorts, his flannel shirt is buttoned up very properly to his neck. His blue eyes leap from Mirka to her father and back again as he cracks jokes and generally holds court. When they are finished, I ask to take his picture.

Mirka laughs. "Only with me, he says." I position them together by the barn wall and do my best to capture the life in the old man's eyes. He fusses to Mirka about his mended sweater. And then we leave him to his morning and find a bench where we can sit while Mirka thumbs through her notebook and lays out the following string of pearls.

Josephus married a woman named Maria and they had one son, Alojz, and one daughter named after her mother. Alojz inherited the family wealth so he was a relatively rich man, with a big house. He was a teacher, very outgoing, but he never much liked Kvačany. He joined the army and became "something more than a soldier." Then he moved to Košice in the east, and then on to Bratislava, where he married and had one son, who must be about my mom's age.

Josephus' daughter Maria married a man from the village and had two boys and a girl. Because the family wealth had gone to her older brother, she was left with very little. Her husband never made much money, and because he could not provide the life Josephus wanted for his daughter, the two men were not friendly. Maria's two boys were both drivers, and both died as young men; the brother who lived longer left behind a wife and two daughters. Maria's daughter, Lubica, also married, and still lives in this town.

The man had said more general things about the region, too. School was not mandatory here until 1963. There were four classes, for children aged six to nine, but it was only for people who could afford it, and most kids were needed in the field. After 1963, children were to go to school between the ages of six and twelve. As for coal mining, only one person from this village ever ventured underground. He went to an operation in the Czech Republic. A fire broke out in the mine and to prevent the fire from spreading, the owners shut down the affected shaft, trapping the men inside. The man was lucky to be returned to Kvačany, and from that time on, mining was dangerous.

I am punch drunk. Ján says Ladislav told him that God must have willed our meeting. While I'm not one to believe such things, right now it doesn't seem an unreasonable proposition.

We have only a limited time before I have to board a train back to Bratislava, so we decide to not look for Lubica but instead to visit the church. It is open because a group of women is cleaning it. They are not keen to let us in, but Ján works his magic and soon we are stepping across a vacuum cleaner cord and crossing the threshold.

There are places so rich they defy memory or even description. Walking into the church in Kvačany is like walking into something that is not quite air. There are perhaps thirty pews. There are fresh flowers throughout. The massive carved altarpieces steal the very words from your tongue. The atmosphere is cold and mouldy.

Catholics made the original painted friezes on the plaster walls. Some time later, when a new Protestant ruler took over the country, the church was converted to Protestantism and the walls were whitewashed. Two hundred years later, it was Catholic again and the friezes were restored. This was the church where Andreas and his family heard mass. Next door, in what is now the rectory, is where he went to school and must have dreamt about the life he would have when the massive church no longer towered above him. I was not permitted to take pictures.

Something tells me they might have turned out blank.

Heading out of Kvačany, I ask Ján what happened during Soviet rule to churches such as the one we have just seen. Were they simply locked up?

"Not for the common people," he says, "but for teachers and state people. When these people wanted their children baptized, it had to be secret." There must be people in Kvačany who don't go to church and for whom it is little more than the big building by the river. But I'd wager there are many more for whom locking that church would have meant war.

Which reminds me that with the exception of some rhetoric to which I have been exposed over the years, I really haven't a clue what communism was like for people who lived it. Was everything provided to everyone who worked? Was there even such a thing as cash?

"Everybody had a job," Ján explains by way of Mirka. "He who didn't want to work went to prison. Everyone had some money but there was not as big difference between people as now. You received money, and you exchanged this for special money for things produced in our country. Then when you wanted, you had to stand in long lines. For oranges, even."

The part about the smaller gap between rich and poor doesn't sound so bad to me. I ask him if common people were better off before or after 1989, when communism ended in Slovakia. He thinks for a moment, then delivers a quick answer to Mirka.

Mirka chuckles. "I will tell you in his words. He says when you are a dog on chain, you are not free, but you are fed. A wolf is free, but has no food. With communism, we are like dog. Now, we are like wolf. You understand?"

We head toward Zuberec and an open-air museum where dwellings and work buildings from throughout the area around Orava district have been dismantled, piece by painstaking piece, and reassembled in a kind of planar archaeology. Ján and I have dropped our pretenses of language and are now communicating with gestures, and the odd attempt at a word in common. But these are the material remnants of farmers — ploughs, mills, water pumps, wood stoves, weaving machines, giant wooden bowls for feeding giant appetites for bread — and this, I think I understand.

On our way back to Dolný Kubín, I ask Mirka to tell him that I have been honoured by this trip. And he thanks me.

After a quick lunch, it's time to head to Kral'ovany so I can catch my train to Bratislava. We have one more stop to make on the way there.

In Parnica, we halt in front of a house with an attached barn and an admirable garden around the side. Mirka's twin aunts — one living in Prague and one still living in Slovakia — meet us at the gate. Ján calls out to the woman bent over in the yard. Mirka's grandmother stands up and waves us in. First things first: an old sandwich and a pat on the head for the dog. Mirka's grandmother is wearing a golf shirt and skirt with an apron. Her white hair is gathered at the nape of her neck in a neat bun. She greets me with a hug.

Mirka and her father show me through the barns, pointing out all the old tools and things for the animals that once lived there before Mirka's grandparents became too old to handle all but a few chickens. Then to the garden. I ask if I can steal a few cherries; Ján breaks off an entire branch and hands it to me. When it starts to rain, we make a break for the kitchen. In the corner is a built-in tile oven, a modern riff on the ones we have just seen in the museum.

The women are busy cutting bread and cheese and sausage, pouring potato chips into bowls, and arranging cookies on plates. Cognac and two bottles of beer appear from another room. One of Mirka's aunts sets out a number of shot glasses.

Na zdravie! Na zdravie! To your health and down the hatch. Mirka's grandfather has a piece of bread to chase it down and stays to the edge of the fray. Mirka and her father relate the details of our travels today, much to everyone's delight. The aunt from Slovakia retrieves a wheel of cheese. "Slovenský," she says as she holds it up for me.

"It is cheese from cow, with salt." Mirka says. "I think you will like it." And I do, very much. Moments later, Mirka's grandmother brings me a clear plastic bag containing what looks like pastry dough.

"Present," she says.

Mirka elaborates. "It is a present for you. Is cheese from sheep, from this area."

There is more talking and eating and drinking. I sit at the table trying to guess from people's tone of voice and the glances in my direction what they're saying, but mostly I cradle my coffee in my hands and feel very much at home.

At the station, Mirka, her father, and mother and I say our good-byes. I give them each a hug, feeling small because I cannot thank them properly for the unbridled kindness they have shown me. We stand on the platform, me with a mound of cheese and a cherry branch sticking out of my bag, waiting for my train.

Perhaps during travel, one is more receptive to meaning. But in a moment straight out of parables and Hollywood endings, as we look toward the tracks, a coal train, full to the gills, rounds the corner, lumbers by, and rattles off into the distance.

[xxiv]

She resurfaces, blinks in the bright sun. The
sounds of her children on the riverbank come
to her. She stares into the blank dome of the sky.

[epilogue]

This story has been under construction in some form or another for more than ten years, which is a bit strange. Mom never spoke of her grandmother; even Grandma barely spoke of her. I certainly wasn't around to meet Rosalia Patalla. Since I was adopted by her descendants, it's not even some hidden genetic compulsion egging me on to find out who she was.

I think Rosalia has haunted me so because she is a part of the creation story of the west. It took me a while to see that because my own family history seemed so mundane. Indeed it is. We have had no powerful political figures, no huge wealth, no streets or towns named after us. We are just like any other family, to borrow a phrase from Aunt Cec.

But as a journalist, I started learning more about the power of story. I learned that every story needs a protagonist. I learned that the protagonist doesn't have to be powerful or rich or smart or beautiful; her job in the story is simply to teach.

For me, this story started as a desire to record my grandmother's memories before she passed away. From there I began trying to coax it into the larger story of immigrant women's experiences in the coal-mining towns of the Crowsnest Pass. At times, I was sorely disappointed by my failures.

But as I was trudging up the hill to Bratislava Castle one muggy July afternoon, it occurred to me that larger social histories are simply filing systems that various authors apply to the bits of raw data that are individual lives. I'm not a historian. I've tried to engage Rosalia as a journalist would. She just happens to have also been the reason my family exists in this time and place.

Recently, a friend (let's call her Sonya) of a friend (let's call her Kathy) died from cancer. Sonya wasn't yet forty, and as I listened to Kathy talk of sitting at her bedside, promising to make sure her two young children were loved and got a good education, I said to Kathy, "I can't believe I get so caught up in my own small problems when Sonya and a million people like her are going through that."

"Monica," she said, "life is a collection of small things. If I ever got to the point where the small things didn't matter, it wouldn't be living at all." At the time I considered it another example of why Kathy is such an extraordinary person. It was good advice for a medical student. Turns out it applies to history, too.

Rosalia — in fact and fiction — is my offering of one small thing.

[acknowledgements]

Many people helped with the research of this book, either by pointing me to written sources or by telling me stories: Caron Townsend and Wendy Zack at the Crowsnest Museum in Coleman; Veronica Fontana, Orestes Serra, Irene Wood, Julie Lant, and John Kinnear. Claudia Cole was the researcher in Victoria I hired to scour the archives. Various members of the Zak clan provided invaluable direction.

My time in Slovakia was utterly dependent on the kindness of strangers, and I was shown incredible kindness by Ján, Slávka, and Miroslava Lietava; Miroslava, Ján, and Melánia Nemčeková; and Martin Banič. George Fodor in Ottawa made it all happen in the first place. Marian Kotrec read things over for me with an eye to all things Slovak.

Speaking of Marian, I have to tell you this story. I was a medical student on an internal medicine team in St. John's in the early months of 2007. I asked my new resident where he was from. "Slovakia," he replied.

"Oh, I was there two years ago," I said. When he asked me why, I told him I had family connections there. Later that night, during a lull in the emergency room, I hazarded a ridiculous question: "Speaking of Slovakia, did you ever meet an internist by the name of Ján Lietava?" He looked at me strangely: "He was my supervisor."

I told him the whole story.

Rosencrantz, like I said.

Books I drew on for my research include: Stanislav J. Kirschbaum's *A History of Slovakia: The Struggle for Survival* (New York: St. Martin's Press, 1995); Melissa Fay Greene's *Last Man Out: The Story of the Springhill Mine Disaster* (Orlando, FL: Harcourt, 2003); Eliane Leslau Silverman's *The Last Best West: Women on the Alberta Frontier: 1880–1930* (Calgary, AB: Fifth House, 1998); Frank Anderson and Art Downs' *Tragedies of the Crowsnest Pass: The Frank Slide* (Surrey, BC: Heritage House, 1983); Wayne Norton and

Tom Langford's (eds.) *A World Apart: The Crowsnest Communities in Alberta and British Columbia* (Kamloops, BC: Plateau Press, 2002); *Crowsnest and Its People Millennium Ed.*, Book III (Coleman, AB: Crowsnest Pass Historical Society, 2000); and Diane Lewis and John Pengelly's (eds.) *Through the Years: A Sociological History of the Ardley, Delburne, and Lousana Areas* (Delburne, AB: Anthony Henday Historical Society, 1980).

Thanks to Stan Dragland for his early suggestion about a possible shape for this book. And to my family, for sharing their stories.

Cecilia Zak passed away before she could read this book. I hope it pays some tribute to her formidable memory and generous spirit.

Monica Kidd was raised in the small town of Elnora, AB. Shortly after moving to Newfoundland in 1998, she began working full-time as a reporter for CBC Radio, where she won numerous awards for news stories and documentaries. She is the author of *Actualities*, a collection of poetry, as well as the novels *The Momentum of Red* and *Beatrice*.

After completing a BSc in Zoology at the University of Calgary and a MSc in Biology at Queen's University, she attended medical school at the Memorial University of Newfoundland. She is currently a medical resident in St. John's, Newfoundland.

Eric Gill designed this book's serif typeface, Joanna, in 1930, and the sans serif typeface, Gill Sans, in 1927. The chapters marked with Roman numerals are set in Journal, which was designed in 1990 by the Slovak designer Zuzana Ličko.